Finns in Michigan

DISCOVERING THE PEOPLES OF MICHIGAN
Arthur W. Helweg, Russell M. Magnaghi, and Linwood H. Cousins, Series Editors

Ethnicity in Michigan: Issues and People
Jack Glazier and Arthur W. Helweg

French Canadians in Michigan
John P. DuLong

African Americans in Michigan
Lewis Walker, Benjamin C. Wilson,
and Linwood H. Cousins

Albanians in Michigan
Frances Trix

Jews in Michigan
Judith Levin Cantor

Amish in Michigan
Gertrude Enders Huntington

Italians in Michigan
Russell M. Magnaghi

Germans in Michigan
Jeremy W. Kilar

Poles in Michigan
Dennis Badaczewski

Dutch in Michigan
Larry ten Harmsel

Asian Indians in Michigan
Arthur W. Helweg

Latinos in Michigan
David A. Badillo

South Slavs in Michigan
Daniel Cetinich

Hungarians in Michigan
Éva V. Huseby-Darvas

Mexicans and Mexican Americans in Michigan
Rudolph Valier Alvarado
and Sonya Yvette Alvarado

Scots in Michigan
Alan T. Forrester

Greeks in Michigan
Stavros K. Frangos

Chaldeans in Michigan
Mary C. Sengstock

Latvians in Michigan
Silvija D. Meija

Arab Americans in Michigan
Rosina J. Hassoun

Irish in Michigan
Seamus P. Metress and Eileen K. Metress

Scandinavians in Michigan
Jeffrey W. Hancks

Cornish in Michigan
Russell M. Magnaghi

Belgians in Michigan
Bernard A. Cook

Copts in Michigan
Eliot Dickinson

Yankees in Michigan
Brian C. Wilson

Finns in Michigan
Gary Kaunonen

Discovering the Peoples of Michigan is a series of publications examining the state's rich multicultural heritage. The series makes available an interesting, affordable, and varied collection of books that enables students and lay readers to explore Michigan's ethnic dynamics. A knowledge of the state's rapidly changing multicultural history has far-reaching implications for human relations, education, public policy, and planning. We believe that Discovering the Peoples of Michigan will enhance understanding of the unique contributions that diverse and often unrecognized communities have made to Michigan's history and culture.

Finns in Michigan

Gary Kaunonen

Michigan State University Press

East Lansing

♾ The paper used in this publication meets the minimum requirements
of ANSI/NISO Z39.48-1992 (R 1997) (Permanence of Paper).

Michigan State University Press
East Lansing, Michigan 48823-5245

Printed and bound in the United States of America.

18 17 16 15 14 13 12 11 10 09   1 2 3 4 5 6 7 8 9 10

ISBN: 978-0-87013-844-7

LIBRARY OF CONGRESS CATALOGING-IN-PUBLICATION DATA
Kaunonen, Gary.
Finns in Michigan / Gary Kaunonen.
p. cm.—(Discovering the peoples of Michigan)
Includes bibliographical references and index.
ISBN 978-0-87013-844-7 (pbk. : alk. paper) 1. Finnish Americans—Michigan—History.
2. Finnish Americans—Michigan—Social conditions. 3. Finnish Americans—Employment—
Michigan—History. 4. Working class—Michigan—History. I. Title.
F575.F5K38 2008
977.4'00494541—dc22
2008029518

Discovering the Peoples of Michigan.

Cover design by Ariana Grabec-Dingman
Book design by Sharp Designs, Lansing, Michigan
Cover photo: The results of a bountiful harvest from a day of picking strawberries in Oskar Bay, Michigan,
ca. 1925. *Finlandia University's Finnish American Historical Archive, Libby Koski-Björklund Collection.*

Michigan State University Press is a member of the Green Press Initiative and is committed to developing and encouraging ecologically responsible publishing practices. For more information
about the Green Press Initiative and the use of recycled paper in book publishing, please visit *www.
greenpressinitiative.org.*

Visit Michigan State University Press on the World Wide Web at *www.msupress.msu.edu*

To Sofia and Niilo,
struggle and work
for a better tomorrow

Contents

Introduction

At times ethnic histories become whitewashed presentations of what we want certain ethnic groups to be; the best elements of an ethnicity's characteristics and recitations of the preferred ideological tenets or the accomplishments of new people living forthright lives in a land of unbounded possibilities. This book will not be one of those endeavors, because to present such a history does not accurately depict the history of the Finns in Michigan. This book intends to be a broad survey of the social and labor history of the Finns in Michigan—inclusive of the good, the bad, and the ugly aspects of the Finnish experience in Michigan.

The story of the Finns in Michigan is ultimately a history of the working class and this book will largely be about those who toiled in the mines, fields, factories, forests, and quarries of Michigan. There was a small but influential business or middle class in Finnish immigrant Michigan and we will certainly examine aspects of their place in Michigan history, but this book will focus on those often overlooked by customary histories. Traditional American histories often discount groups that did not support idealized visions of America. People that did not represent the idyllic "American" are impugned and events that run counter to the celebration of America's march toward prominence are marginalized or disregarded.

One such tale that abounds is that Suomi College (currently Finlandia University) was and is the "only college founded by Finns in America."[1] This particular statement was culled from a 1986–89 Suomi College Class Catalog, but this claim was a staple of the college's promotional literature for decades, and even today Finlandia University states in its 2007 University Course Catalog that, "it [Finlandia University] remains the only university founded by Finns."[2] While the latter statement is true, Finlandia is the only *university* in America founded by Finns, the former assertion that Suomi College was the only college founded by Finns in America is abjectly false.

There was at least one other institution of higher learning founded by the Finns in America. This college began as a Finnish Lutheran school in Minneapolis, but became a college of proletarian education in 1906 known as the *Työvaen Opisto*, or Work People's College, in Smithville, Minnesota (now Duluth).[3] This myth, that Suomi College was and is the only institution of higher learning founded by Finns in America, has persisted because at some point in Suomi College's history someone or some group of people decided to disregard a segment of history they found disagreeable or did not do the necessary research to "find" the history of the Work People's College.

Conventional histories ignore the Work People's College because it espoused and taught a radical proletarian curriculum. Many of the instructors at Work People's College were members of the Industrial Workers of the World (IWW) or "Wobblies" and thus in direct conflict with ecclesiastical, middle-class Finnish immigrants. Disregard for the Work People's College's history might lead some to believe that the Work People's College was a small, insignificant school, but the Work People's College often had a higher enrollment than Suomi College and occupied a very prominent place in Finnish America. In 1915, for example, the Work People's College had eighty-eight students, a twelve-member board of directors, eight professors, a large central building with classrooms, dorms, and an on-site publishing company. Suomi College had the same physical structures, nine faculty members and seventy-two students.[4] At this time, the student population, instructors, and physical facilities were almost the same at both institutions, but the Work People's College's place in Finnish American history has been omitted by some, perceivably because of ideological bias.

The Suomi Synod/Suomi College headquartered in Hancock, Michigan, was historically an extension of Finland's Evangelical Lutheran Church in

The Copper Country Giant—Big Louie Moilanen

Perhaps no Finn in Michigan could have left a bigger mark on the state than the Copper Country Giant, Big Louie Moilanen—all 8-foot, four-hundred-some-odd pounds of him. Big Louie was born in Finland in 1885. Louie grew to a regular-sized man by age nine and by his eighteenth birthday, Louie was around 8'1". The Moilanen family lived on a farm outside a small copper mining location north of Hancock, Michigan, known as Boston. Louie ventured from the farm to work in a mine, but grew tired of the utterly cramped quarters. He then found work in (of course) the circus, as a curiosity in traveling shows including the world-renowned Ringling Brothers and Barnum and Bailey Circus.[*]

Copper Country Giant Big Louie Moilanen stands next to a normal sized man, ca. 1910. Courtesy of Finlandia University's Finnish American Historical Archive, Historic Photograph Collection.

Shy by nature, Louie's stint with the circus was not a happy or very long affair. Business cards bemoaned the loneliness he found at the big top: "Do not spurn me . . . a rag-time millionaire am not married willing to be . . . I never flirt . . . looking for someone to love." While Louie was out on the road his father died, and this, and perhaps loneliness, brought Louie back to the Copper Country. After another stretch on the farm, Louie headed to Hancock to own a bar. Could there have been a more formidable bouncer? His control over the bar must have been considerable, because in 1911 he won election as justice of the peace for Hancock Township. By 1913, the Giant's health was deteriorating, and he died on September 16, 1913. His casket was reportedly nine feet long and three feet wide.[†]

---

[*] Houghton County Historical Society, *Big Louie Moilanen: Giant of the Copper Country* (Lake Linden, Mich.: John H. Forster Press, 1995), 2–4.
[†] Ibid., 4–8.

America and was often at loggerheads with socialist factions of the politico-labor movement. This split between religious people and socialist elements was certainly not unique to the Finns in Michigan, but was perhaps more pronounced because the socialist Finn elements in Michigan and America occupied a very prominent place in the immigrant culture and often acted as a dialectical foil to the Suomi Synod and College. This historical split in the Finnish immigrant culture is illustrative of a major theme in Finnish American history; some folks, including myself, refer to Finns as the largest dysfunctional family in America. While this is a somewhat tongue-in-cheek statement, it emits a certain truth, and evidence in this book will support that assertion.

The fractioning in Michigan Finns' cultural organizations has subsided for the most part over time and in some instances the divides that once separated have become insignificant. An excellent example of the healing that has taken place in Finnish America is the *Finnish American Reporter*. The Työmies Society, a communistic group with connections to Hancock, Michigan, began publishing the *Finnish American Reporter* in 1986 as an ideologically and politically neutral forum for the discussion of ethnic heritage and history. When the Työmies Society began to experience terminal problems sustaining readership of their main publication, *Työmies-Eteenpäin,* in the mid-1990s, they deeded the *Finnish American Reporter* to their old ideological adversary, Suomi College, in 1999.[5] Time certainly heals most wounds and the maintenance of ethnic identity in this case overcame former bitter ideological wrangling.

The preceding introduction was a broad contextual sketch of the topics in play for this history of the Finns in Michigan. In this book, we will endeavor to put flesh on the bones of Michigan Finns' historical skeletons by probing the intricacies of immigration, labor, and ideology. The history of the Finns in Michigan consists of a vibrant, diverse, dramatic, and at times deeply quarrelsome account of a people whose contributions to the state left an indelible mark on its history.

Finns Out, "Jack-pine Savages" In

To many of us today, it would seem almost inconceivable to leave your family, travel thousands of miles to a new land, and never see your relatives or country of birth again. Yet, many emigrant Finns did just this. The specific reasons for this often frenzied movement to America were complex. For some, America was a "bread and butter" economic decision, they needed food to live and Finland was not providing it, so they took a chance on what America had to offer. For others, America was a chance to start over and begin a new life. Still others saw America as a place to get rich and then travel back to the homeland as a wealthy person. Some left to avoid conscription into the Russian czar's army. Others came to own a piece of land they could call their own, and a few likely came purely for adventure.[6]

In all, roughly 308,000 emigrants departed Finland for America between 1865 and 1914.[7] Most of the emigrants from Finland were literally the archetypical hungry, poor masses yearning to breathe free. In the 1860s, Finland experienced a series of crop failures that turned the rural countryside into barren badlands. Finland maintained, possibly because of its subjugation by Swedish and Russian imperial kings from 1325 to 1917, a permanent non-landed class. In 1870, over 80 percent of the Finnish population was landless, comprised of hired laborers, dependent cottagers, and tenant farmers.[8] Rural Finns depended heavily on the land, and these agriculturally focused people had little in the way of economic prospects after the blights. Many Finns from the western and northern agricultural provinces saw life in America or in the southern urban centers of Finland as the only remedy to their situation.[9]

For Finland's very large peasant class, economic conditions in the homeland were at best difficult and at worst unlivable, but social and cultural subjugation under Swedish aristocrats living in Finland and absentee czarist Russian bureaucrats was too much to bear for many Finns. The Swedish monarchy ruled Finland from 1362 until 1809. Sweden lost possession of Finland in the mess that was the Napoleonic Wars. Russia seized upon Sweden's preoccupation in these wars and annexed Finland into the Russian empire in 1809. Finland remained a possession of the czar from 1809 to 1917, when the Bolshevik revolution provided Finland the opportunity to declare its independence.[10]

The Finnish peasant class, the crofters, tenant farmers, and dependent lodgers toiled under a sort of imperially sponsored serfdom for over 550 years. Sweden fought many of its imperial wars with sparring partner Russia in Finland from the late 1500s until 1809. Burnt crops, war-inspired taxes, and allegiance to the Swedish crown loomed large over Finnish lives.[11] With Russian control, the Grand Duchy of Finland gained a semblance of autonomy. Finns established their own government within the Russian empire, known as the Finnish Diet, which first convened in 1809, and later reestablished regular sessions in 1863.[12]

Finns generally enjoyed a degree of freedom under Russian czars until the late 1890s. In 1898, Czar Nicholas II appointed Nikolai Ivanovich Bobrikov as governor general of Finland. Bobrikov began a series of Russification programs that created a bitter taste on many Finnish palates. A group of Finns responded to Bobrikov's Russification programs by assassinating him in 1904. Bobrikov's "years of oppression" took their toll and resulted in dissolution of the Finnish Diet, industrialization of Finnish countryside agriculture for Russian markets, and conscription of many Finns into the Russian army. This created a large group of laborers with no tie to the land and a large population of "draft dodgers" with a fledgling proletarian consciousness. In addition to displaced rural folk, radical political elements initiated anti-imperialist movements in Finland's southern urban centers, inciting the 1905 general strike. The czarist government exiled or precipitated the emigration of many of these southern Finnish radicals.[13]

Immigration

The common perception is that many Finns settled in parts of America where the environment reminded them of home. This assertion is largely false. Economic opportunity, or rather the perception of opportunity, likely pulled many Finns to places in America . . . places that had economic prospects in the form of demand for unskilled labor in American industry. Michigan at the beginning of the twentieth century was one such place, and by 1930 Michigan had amassed 74,229 foreign-born and American-born Finns. This was the most of any state or province in North America.[14] It was the copper and iron mines, the huge tracts of white pine forests, and perhaps above all else, the cheap land that beckoned many Finnish emigrants to Michigan in search of economic opportunity.

For many Finnish immigrants, stories of America included streets of gold and food for everyone. Finns living in America wrote their friends and relatives of the good fortune in the New World, but tales of success and plenty were often misleading. Finnish immigration agents and companies hungry for strong-backed, weak-pocketed immigrants aggrandized stories of opportunity and wealth, hoping to make a quick profit by volume of immigrants shipped and employed. Some of these agents acted as unscrupulous traffickers of men, women, and children, advising of opportunity, yet turning over their collections of immigrants to companies needing a quick influx of cheap human capital.[15]

Jobs in America, for most Finnish immigrants, meant industrial work, and Finns came to America and Michigan as a sort of tabula rasa, most being wholly unfamiliar with the way of industrial life and work or the wage system. This was, however, not true with the first, small tide of Finnish immigrants who found industrial employment in Michigan's Copper Country. A group of ethnic Finns, known as the Kven, settled in northern Norway between 1825 and 1865. In this remote region of Norway, these Finns sought employment as fishermen and miners. When employment at Norwegian mines began to peter out, many Finns followed Norwegians and Swedes to America on the invite of labor recruiters from the Quincy Mine in Hancock, Michigan.[16]

The first small group of Finns from the northern Norwegian mines of Kaafjord and Alten arrived in Michigan around 1864, and a larger group of approximately thirty arrived in 1865. These early path-finding immigrants filled

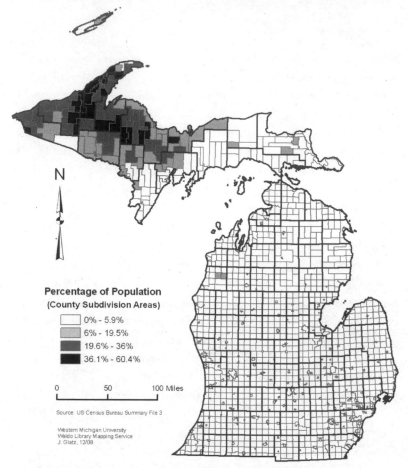

Distribution of Michigan's population claiming Finnish ancestry (2000).

the need for labor in the mines while many former Michigan miners were fighting in the Civil War.[17] These "Scandinavians" found lodging in Quincy's ethnically separated ghetto, Swedetown. Unlike many of Quincy's company housing locations, which featured wood-framed houses, Swedetown was a ramshackle assortment of small, unkempt log houses located miles away from Quincy's industrial site.[18] This was the first Finnish experience with industrial Michigan.

From this early trickle of immigrants into the state, the floodgates opened in the mid-1880s and a deluge of Finns into Michigan ensued. The Copper

Country received the lion's share of immigrants, but the Marquette, Gogebic, and Menominee iron ranges received healthy doses of Finns as well. As aforementioned, many of Michigan's Finnish immigrants were agriculturalists. Working in the vast caverns of Michigan's underground copper and iron mines must have been a shock to the system. Instead of working under blue skies and in green fields, Finns were now toiling in relative darkness, often surrounded by the stale odor of human sweat and blasting powder. Perhaps the worst aspect of mine labor was that Finns now were dictated to by the tick-tock of a clock and not the rising and setting of the sun.

Industrial areas in Michigan were very isolated and overrun with young men. These men got homesick or lonely and in this wake, industrial boomtown communities became wild backwaters of drinking, prostitution, and vice. Women of the marrying variety were at a premium, and when the occasional lady came on the scene, anxious slack-jawed admirers courted her post-haste.[19] A letter from Viktor Ollikainen, written to Hilja Fraki, a woman he met while making the voyage from Finland to the United States, indicated that life in the iron-mining town of Ishpeming was lonely:

> And have you been suited a lot and do you have a fiancé at this moment? Why don't you come here to Ishpeming? It is fun here and lots of boys and a few girls. Time passes here well so nobody will feel bored here. It would be nice for you to meet us some time. There are three boys in this house and we all came on the same journey, John Housu and John Motti also asked me to send you lots of regards. . . . Well, you may get bored while reading this story of mine if I still continue. So, I will finish this time and hope that you don't mind me writing to you. Please forgive me and answer to this letter and please send me your picture. I will send you mine. So long and feel good.[20]

Life in industrial America could be lonely, but also very short. The industrial work was very labor intensive and fraught with danger. If the letter is any indication, Viktor seems in a hurry to marry; asking Hilja if she had a fiancé . . . perhaps Viktor knew that with mining came the possibility of a quick death. Industrial America was a new horizon for many immigrant Finns; a lifestyle that few could avoid as they attempted to make their way in a new world.

In some instances men leaving Finland did so without their wives and children. As Sandra Sarkela of Negaunee remembers:

> He (Sandra's father) left from America on May 28th and came to Finland to get us because my mother would never agree to come alone with me here (to Negaunee). He had to come to Finland to get us. . . . Well then we decided to sell the farm and the furniture and we left in 1911 to sail to America.[21]

Inevitably, some families were never made whole, as fathers stayed in America. Some men even remarried. An especially riveting tale occurred in Michigan's copper mining capital, Red Jacket (Calumet):

> The sensation among the Finnish people on Pine Street is the case of Herman Dahl, who has been living here for several months with a woman he claimed was his legitimate wife.
>
> Yesterday his first wife and daughter, a girl about 16 years of age, arrived from the Old Country and at once hunted up her faithless husband. She found him and after some talk between them he agreed to leave his second wife and live with his first wife. Although he had done her a great wrong, she was willing to forgive him if he would now take care of his family of six children.[22]

Things seemed to be in place for a flawless family reconciliation until Herman and wife number one headed to the bank to draw out some money. This is where they met wife number two, who had already drawn out the entire $165.00 of "Herman's" bank account. As the story concludes, "Right here is where the trouble began. Herman wanted the money, but wife #2 claimed the money was as much hers as it was her husband's."[23]

We should note that Calumet, Michigan, was of special significance for the Finnish immigrant population. The mighty Calumet and Hecla copper mine was a large employer of Finns for some time. Additionally, very notable Finnish exiles from all spectrums of the sociopolitical sphere turned to Calumet for refuge after being expelled from Finland by the Russian czar. In 1904, Carl Gustav Mannerheim, future leader of the Finns versus the Soviets in the famous Winter War and eventual president of Finland, sought

Kaleva, Michigan

Even places that seemingly had no connection to industrialized Michigan had an industrial connection for Finns. Kaleva, Michigan, in Manistee County, one of the few Finn rural agricultural settlements in Michigan's Lower Peninsula, has a strong twofold connection to heavy industry. The first connection came before Kaleva's founding and includes the "iron horse." After the Chicago and Western Michigan Railroad Company and the Manistee and Northeastern Company had a log-chopping contest to hasten the laying of track for their rail lines, a vast area of contemporary Manistee County was a "veritable wasteland and vale of sorrows."[*]

Into this wasteland strode Jacob E. Saari, a Finnish land agent for the New York National Land Association. After changing the small settlement's name from Manistee Crossing to Kaleva (a name associated with the Finnish national epic), "Settler Jack" as he was known began to sell off wasteland for $5.00 an acre. Settler Jack's adept promotion of Kaleva's cutover barren lands made Kaleva the largest Finnish agricultural settlement in Michigan. After initial struggles with its poor soil and dry summers, Kaleva was soon a prospering agricultural community with a church, a temperance society, the *Siirtolainen* (Immigrant) Publishing Company, and a thriving cucumber-growing industry, the "fruits" of which were shipped to a Pittsburgh pickle factory.[†]

Kaleva Finns' other interaction with heavy industry was much less celebratory. A significant number of Kaleva's settlers came from Hanna, Wyoming, on the tail of a horrible mining accident. Hanna, a coal-mining town on the Union Pacific Railway, saw a group of Finns die in a mine cave-in. Apparently, after the disaster, some of the Finnish folks in Hanna had had enough of mining coal and left the area to settle in Kaleva, possibly because a number of Finns from neighboring Carbon, Wyoming, had settled in Kaleva previously.[‡]

[*] Holmio, *Finns in Michigan*,163–64.
[†] Ibid.
[‡] Suomi Synod Collection, Kaleva, Michigan, Manuscript Collection Boxes A-91a and A-91b, Membership Rolls, Finlandia University's Finnish American Historical Archive, Hancock, Michigan.

exile in Calumet. In the same year, Carl Canth, social reformer and son of famed feminist and labor activist Minna Canth, also laid low in Calumet for a time.[24]

While on the surface Michigan presented opportunity, to many Finnish immigrants the state became a large jail cell. Some immigrants were caught in the remote industrial cities or isolated logging camps of Michigan, penniless and homesick, longing for the place they once called home. Elou Kiviranta, a rural poet and traditional healer from Nisula, Michigan, captured the longing of wayward Finns for their homeland in a poem titled "The Memory of Finland":

> *I am remembering sweet Finland*
> *It cannot come out of my heart*
> *I cannot forget it.*
> *I was glorifying it recently.*
> *There is no other country on earth*
> *where the brightness is so clear*
> *the air is so fresh.*
> *So sweet a smell in every place*
> *exuberant trees around the home.*
> *Those I cannot ever forget*
> *The light summer nights*
> *Nature as a whole*
> *that decorates my father's land . . .*
>
> *The fields of farmer were waving smoothly*
> *And green fields of grass*
> *Warm wind of summer was blowing*
> *All the lakes were glittering bright*
> *So tender were the banks of rivers*
> *The sweetness of Finland*
> *The irreplaceable feeling*
> *I always carry in my heart.*
> *That glory I have lost forever*
> *From America I am never going to see it again.*[25]

In its worst application, the soil of Michigan became a Finnish immigrant's grave. Thousands of Finnish immigrants died in the mines and woods of Michigan. Because many never became citizens, it is often difficult to get an accurate account of the numbers.

Many Finnish immigrants returned to Finland; some made the voyage between Finland and the United States several times. Defining real numbers in re-emigration is difficult, as cultural historian Keijo Virtanen writes: "Analyzing re-emigration involves breaking much new ground because there are only a few studies dealing with the subject and must involve the use of quantitative data to measure the moment of emigration as well as the moment of re-emigration. . . . But reliable statistics on which to base a quantitative study are difficult to find." [26] Some researchers of Finnish re-emigration put the number of those returning from America to Finland at one-third of the immigrant population, but Virtanen opines that the number is closer to one-fifth. Virtanen also asserts that re-emigration was often contingent upon cyclical factors such as employment. *If* there was work in America, there was reason to stay; if not, perhaps a return trip was in order. [27]

Jack-pine Savages

In America, Finns acquired a definite outsider's status. Even though they often looked like their non-Finn neighbors in America with blonde hair and blue eyes, Finns had a strange way of talking and an even stranger set of socio-cultural practices. Whereas a Swedish or Norwegian Germanic-speaking miner could somewhat understand a mining captain speaking English (another language of Germanic origin), no one could understand the Finn. Finnish is not in the Indo-European language family; it is in the Finno-Ugrian family, and this made communication with Indo-European-speaking persons very difficult.

To outsiders, Finns had very strange socio-cultural practices. In one ritual, an entire family walked naked into a super-heated building to throw water on rocks and sit in the steam produced by the practice . . . the sauna. Imagine . . . men seeing women in the buff; this was unacceptable behavior for upstanding, refined Victorian men and women in America. Additionally, Finnish women often worked alongside the men in the fields, another

Adding to this "savage" perception were the actions of a few drunken, out of control men and perhaps women. In Michigan's industrial communities, Finns became well known for their knife fighting skills, especially after a long day of binge drinking in the local saloon. As often happens, the actions of a few reflected poorly upon the larger community and Finns in general became known as incorrigible, sometimes brutal drunks. The episodes of knife fighting and violence angered almost all Finns in Michigan, with the possible exception of those engaged in the events. Most Finns in Michigan were law-abiding folks looking to better their lot in the New World and not cut it up into shreds.[30]

Finns at Work in Michigan: Heavy Industry

ike many newcomers to America, Finnish immigrants had to toil in the worst jobs, often on the lowest levels of the labor hierarchy. In mines, Finns were for the most part "grunt labor." In the woods, the constant fear of widow makers (giant hanging branches suspended in tree tops) crashing down from overhead incited a wary temperament in many Finns, but these jobs in heavy industry had interesting unintended consequences.

For many Finns work in the heavy industries had a unifying power. Work in mines, industrial forests, and later factories forced Finns get to know other ethnicities. It made Finns learn, at the very least, parts of the English language. It also made them more receptive to seeing themselves as a part of an American workforce, with all the benefits and burdens of that distinction. To be sure, they likely spoke Finn in their homes, but in the workplace, there was at least a small taste of what it meant to be in America and what it was like to be an American. This process of Americanization was important and conceivably occurred most frequently through labor in Michigan's heavy industries.

Lest we romanticize the lot of hard laboring Finns too much, almost assuredly there were Finn slackers as well, but for the most part Finns were respected laborers. While Finns were respected as workers, they were also suspected supporters of organized labor. After a string of wildcat strikes

"Finglish"

As Finns in America became increasingly involved with non-Finnish populations, a unique phenomenon occurred. A non-Finnish, yet non-English language developed, a Finnish-English pidgin that helped Finnish immigrants navigate in an English-speaking world. The pidgin became lovingly known as "Finglish"; not quite English, but yet different from Finnish.

Finglish likely first came into use in the mines, as this was one of the first places of interaction between Finns and non-Finns. Oftentimes Finglish words developed to describe technical terms that did not exist in Finland. For example, the Finglish word for mine became "maini," boss became "paasi," trammer became "trammari" and an ore skip car became "skippa."[*]

As Finns became increasingly involved with non-Finns, Finglish could often be the root of humorous interactions. Take, for instance, this circa 1935 dialogue between a Finn farmer who ordered a manure spreader through a cooperative store in Paynesville, Michigan, and a telephone operator. The order for the manure bucket went from the co-op to a wholly American, English-speaking farm implement company in Duluth, Minnesota. The implement company had taken some time in filling the farmer's order. So, thoroughly disgusted, the farmer picked up the old crank telephone in the co-op store and proceeded to voice this complaint to the person on the other end: "(Name of company) vas madder you, my sit pucket pisnes no come."[†] Then the irritated farmer hung up the phone. Perhaps being unfamiliar with the telephone systems of the day, the farmer did not recognize that he was likely talking to a telephone board operator in

and suspicious fires at the Calumet and Hecla mines in the late nineteenth and early twentieth centuries, Jim MacNaughton, manager of the copper mining giant, wrote the commissioner of immigration at Ellis Island and the United States Department of Labor, "We do not want Finlanders." This was the status of many Finnish immigrant laborers: respected but suspected. Using this framework, we will look at Finns working in Michigan's heavy industry.[31]

the Upper Peninsula that would in turn connect him with the business and not someone at the actual farm implement company in Duluth.

A quick delve into heavily anglicized Finglish comes from Heino A. "Hap" Puotinen's series of books on the phenomenon written beginning in the late 1960s. An excerpt from Hap's writings:

> Tvinkol, tvinkol, lirol star,
>
> Hau I vunner vat juu are;
>
> Op apove ta vorlt so hai,
>
> Like tat taimon in ta skai.‡

Some informal analysis has even noted that the lack of prepositions in the "Yooper" dialect comes directly from the lack of prepositional phrases in Finn-ish. For example, a sentence such as, "We went to the store" becomes, "We go store" in the Upper Peninsula informal dialect. This is perhaps a direct result of the Finglish phenomenon and the application of preposition-free Finnish syntax. Finglish has become more anglicized over time, and to some extent "folksy," but its current application does not underscore its great historic importance: it signified the Americanization of Finns through language that occurred due to the need to communicate within American industry.

* Niemi, Clemens. *Americanization of the Finnish People in Houghton County, Michigan,* http://www.genealogia. Fi/emi/art.article241e.htm, 7.
† Beatrice Meyers oral history interview, non-transcribed interviews, Oral History Collection, Box 26, conducted by Gary Kaunonen and Hannu Heinilä, July 27, 2006, Chassell, Michigan, Finnish American Historical Archive, Finlandia University, Hancock, Michigan.
‡ Heino A. "Hap" Puotinen, *Sauna-Pukki* (Iron River, Mich.: Reporter Publishing Company), 13.

Mining

A survey of Finn workers in Michigan's extractive industry is as good a place as any to begin the examination of laboring Finns. In descending order, Finns occupied the heavily industrialized mining counties of Houghton, Marquette, Gogebic, and Menominee.[32] It is no surprise that these heavily industrialized mining areas attracted large numbers of unskilled Finn laborers to feed the appetite of America as it industrialized in the late nineteenth and early twentieth centuries. Into this industrial world Finns came and found that the mining environment was, "a highly structured company-corporate environment, complete with its well defined occupational hierarchy, inflexible working hours, established salary scales, regimentation and hazardous working conditions. It (mine work) stood in stark contrast to the predominantly personal, folk-agrarian milieu the Finns had left behind."[33]

Houghton County was the predominate area of copper production during the boom time of the Copper Country. Mining companies like the Calumet and Hecla, Quincy, and Copper Range employed massive numbers of Finnish immigrants. In the first decade of the twentieth century, as the Copper Country mines added workers they struggled to compete with surging copper mines in Montana, Alaska, the southwestern United States, and overseas. Finnish immigrant workers toiled in Houghton County's aging copper mines, some of which had been in operation since the 1840s and plunged to depths of over 9,000 feet by 1920. Finn mine workers often worked ten-hour days, six days a week in the lowest-paying jobs, with an equally low amount of prestige. In 1900, there were roughly 7,250 foreign-born Finns in Houghton County, and that number jumped to 11,500 by 1910.[34] Of course not all Finns worked in the mines, but most of Houghton County's Finns worked as trammers, timbermen, or general laborers in the dark caverns of Houghton County's underground world.

For much of the late nineteenth and early twentieth century Finns joined Italian and eastern European workers on the lowest levels of the labor pecking order as Cornish, German, and American mining captains and miners dictated the pounding industrial rhythm of the mine workings. Added to the poor pay, low prestige, and backbreaking labor there was constant danger in Copper Country mines. From 1905 to 1911, thousand-ton rock falls, electrocution, hundred-foot falls down shafts, and fires killed mine workers in the Copper Country at the rate of a little over one person a week. More staggering, between 1900 and 1909, 511 workers died in the Copper Country mines. From 1900 until the shutdown of mining operations in the Copper Country in the mid-1940s, the Finnish workforce registered the largest number of dead workers, tallying 475 deaths in Copper Country mines.[35]

Newspaper reports listed the mine dead, many of whom were Finns:

This is the result, so far as known, of the explosion of five tons of dynamite yesterday morning at the eighth level of No. 3 shaft, North Kearsarge (mine north of Calumet). The entire mine is now sealed up, in an effort to smother the flames which are licking up the timbers . . . only one dead body is on the surface . . . Five men, William Pollitt, Jr., Peter Savala, John Karvela, Henry Missila and Matt Kaskala, are still missing, and there is practically no doubt they are in the burning mine, dead.[36]

As we have noted, the Calumet and Hecla Mine got out of the business of hiring new Finnish laborers by 1910. Quincy Mine, on the other hand, depended on Finns, employing them as the largest ethnic population in its shafts from 1890 to 1909.[37] After about 1900, the relative peace between Copper Country mining companies and Finnish laborers began to disintegrate. The Finns entering the Copper Country labor pool after this time had been to some extent radicalized by Bobrikoff's Russification programs and the absentee landlord Czar Nicholas II. Many Finnish immigrants were determined not to accept the corporate paternalism of absentee copper company landlords in the Keweenaw Peninsula, which had become known to Finns affectionately as "*kupparisaari*" or copper island.[38]

A rash of strikes in the Copper Country beginning in 1904 and ending in 1914 were led by or highly participated in by Finns. Early wildcat strikes began the push to organize the Copper Country mines. In 1906 Quincy Mining Company management blamed Finns for a strike and two Finns were shot dead in a Rockland, Michigan, strike, and in 1913 and 1914 Finns participated and to some extent led a district-wide strike that brought the shiny million-dollar machinery of the Copper Country companies to a standstill.[39]

The 1913–14 strike was a monumental showdown between monopoly capital and organized labor, with both sides putting everything they had into the event. The mining companies brought in hired security, or "gun hounds" as the strikers knew them. The Michigan National Guard also bivouacked around various mines at the invitation of mine managers to protect life and property, making the Copper Country an armed encampment. The strikers and the Western Federation of Miners union brought in Mother Jones, the famous eighty-plus-year-old labor organizer, and Clarence Darrow, the renowned progressive lawyer.[40]

The strike was a bitter nine-month battle between workers and companies, but for Finns it was an even more bitter battle between Finns who supported the mining company sentiment and their labor-organizing counterparts. At this point, the divide between Suomi College, which generally supported the company position, and those in the labor movement materialized creating bitter feelings on both sides of the divide for decades to come.[41]

The absolute low point of the strike occurred on December 24, 1913. At a multi-ethnic Christmas Eve party for strikers' families in Calumet's Italian Hall, roughly seventy-three people lost their lives in a stampede from the second floor of the hall down a steep staircase to street level. Approximately fifty children and around fifty Finnish persons died in the disastrous event. Shrouded in mystery, exactly what happened on that fateful Christmas Eve and how many people actually died will likely never be known. Striking factions blamed a pro-company group known as the Citizen's Alliance for the horror, and the Finnish immigrant labor newspaper, *Työmies* (Working Man) trumpeted this accusation. The Houghton County sheriff arrested many of *Työmies'* staff for printing this viewpoint, but most of those arrested were later released.[42]

The events of Italian Hall were an exclamation and in essence the concluding event signaling a downturn in the momentum of the strike, as many of the striking workers reentered the mines by April 1914. For the most part, strikers' demands of better wages, better working conditions, and job security, all bread-and-butter issues, were addressed, but recognition of the WFM was not forthcoming, leaving the Copper Country a bastion of mining company influence into the 1940s. It is of note that when the Copper Country mineworkers organized in 1943 through the International Union of Mine, Mill and Smelter Workers, a Finnish American named Gene Saari led the efforts.[43]

While the Copper Country was certainly an early home to many Finns, as news of jobs in Michigan's iron mines spread through the immigrant community, many decided to try their luck with ferrous mining. Finns became a well represented ethnic group in Michigan's iron ore extraction centers. As in the Copper Country, the bulk of Finnish immigrants to the Marquette Range worked as laborers in the mines. As an example, of 1,804 Finns in Ishpeming in 1907, 908 were laboring in iron ore mines. Next to the Copper Country, the Marquette Range became home to the largest Finnish immigrant population.

Iron miners in cage at the Hartford Mine, Negaunee, Michigan, ca. 1904. Amerikan Albumi.

This migration from the Copper Country to Michigan's iron ranges was no random happenstance.

Finnish immigrants used Finnish-language newspapers as a means of communication, and Finns let other Finns know through the printed word the exact trails to travel to find work. In 1880, the Finnish-language newspaper *Amerikan Suomalainen* suggested that Finns begin their search for labor at the Michigamme Mine, then try the Champion or Kingston mines, then the Humboldt. If no work was available there they were advised to try the Republic, and if that mine failed to produce a job, a Finn should, "travel always to Ishpeming and Negaunee, which is the county's (Marquette) center and largest place of employment."[44]

We have described the Copper Country as wild and wooly in its early days. It appears that the Marquette Range was its equal or perhaps its successor.

As Holmio penned, "If life was raw in the Copper Country, it was even more so in iron-mining towns. The majority of men lived in rooming houses which were also called 'flop houses,' and the only gathering places were saloons."[45] Holmio imparts that the prominence of drinking establishments could not go unnoticed, citing the "Finlander" saloons on Ishpeming's Pearl Street. Additionally, he wrote that "Negaunee is between Marquette and Ishpeming. . . . The saloons and churches there symbolized the conflict between good and evil."[46] No matter what the perceived ecclesiastical consequences were for either establishment type, they were equal in the eyes of at least one entity, the heavy red dust that settled on the Marquette Range each spring. The landscape of Marquette Range cities took on a distinctive reddish hue, and in addition to the saloons and churches covered in the red dust, the rows of cookie-cutter company houses took on the same hue.[47]

Life in the rows of company homes was less than idyllic. As Ernie Ronn, a third-generation Finnish American miner who lived on Ann Street in Negaunee, described in 52 *Steps Underground: An Autobiography of a Miner:*

> For my first five years, my world was mostly confined to the thirty-one houses between the Big Hill and Maki's Hill . . . everyone of these houses was within 200 feet of the Athens and Negaunee Mines.
>
> With the exception of one house, all were owned by the mining companies . . . monthly rent for each family ranged from five dollars to thirteen dollars. Electricity and water averaged another three dollars to five dollars per month. Lots were fifty by one hundred feet. Most had two-story barns and an outhouse, in addition to the house. The barns were partitioned so that each family had a place to store winter fuel and to shelter their cows. Because of the limited size of the lots, there was no way of relocating an outhouse if the hole underneath was full. This meant that the outhouse would be built in a corner of the lot on the alley side, and the hole underneath dug deep to avoid any possibility of ever filling up.[48]

If the Marquette Range failed to provide employment, the aforementioned 1880 *Amerikan Suomalainen* article proposed, "Step onto the train at Negaunee and travel to neighboring Menominee County [later split into Dickinson County] which recently was discovered to be rich in iron, and where there are already a dozen mines, in some of which work already 800 men, as for example, in the Norway and Quinnesec Mines, in which every man always finds work."[49] As previously stated, the mines of the Menominee Range had far fewer Finns in their employ, but according to the author of the newspaper article, finding work there was not a problem.

As Leonard Lahti described in an oral history interview, the mine conditions in Iron County's section of the Menominee Range left something to be desired. His father worked the mines as an immigrant, rooming at Vehelia's boarding house in Iron River. From his father's recollections, Leonard described a Menominee Range mine as such: "Yes, they (the Menominee Range mines) were quite rough according to what [my dad] said. It was cold and awfully wet and dangerous. The bosses insisted that the guys go to work in very dangerous places."[50]

The Mansfield Mine in Crystal Falls was one such dangerous place where approximately ten Finns and eighteen other mineworkers died in 1893:

> The shafts of the mine were located on the west bank of the Michigamme River, with the working portion of the mine laid under the river. The first level was 35 feet below the bed of the river. The other levels, five in number, ran parallel with the first. The sixth or bottom level was 428 feet below the surface of the water. All the levels had been stoped out, except for the sixth, leaving only timbers and pillars of ore to bear the tremendous weight of the floors above. The generally accepted cause of the accident was that the timbers on the fifth level gave way and allowed the levels above, and last the river, to crash down. Forty-eight men descended the shaft that Thursday night. Twenty men escaped while the remaining 28 died.[51]

To the northwest of the Menominee Range, the youngest of Michigan's extractive regions opened in 1881. The Gogebic Iron Range was the last of Michigan's iron mining districts to begin production and had Finnish immigrants in its mines almost from the beginning. Ironwood, Michigan, was home to a number of Finn workers early in its life as the central social hub in this iron-mining district. With this early start in Ironwood, Finns began organizing cultural, religious, and social groups very early and to some extent thwarted the most rowdy of the area's inebriated malcontents. Churches, temperance groups, and labor organizations administered to the spiritual and social needs of the many Finn miners who worked the Ashland, Norrie, East Norrie, Aurora, Pabst, and Newport mines.[52]

Frank Walli, son of a Finnish immigrant tailor in Ironwood and nephew of two uncles who worked the Ironwood area mines, recalled a labor organization oriented toward elevating the moral compass of miners in Ironwood:

> In 1919 I attended the affairs of the hall (Palace Labor Hall) . . . the cultural activities. I joined the youth sports group and later on as I got older and got into high school, I joined all the cultural activities then . . . the band, the orchestra, mixed chorus and men's chorus and naturally the athletic club and the drama group.
>
> Well that more or less got me into mass activity and of course the lectures, I attended all the speakers and discussion groups . . . educational groups down there (at the Hall), I'd ask all kinds of questions.[53]

Perhaps because of the organizational activity in Ironwood's various groups, the Michigan side of the Gogebic Range was seemingly more tame than other Michigan iron range communities, but cross the Montreal River into Hurly, Wisconsin, and life on the Wisconsin side of the Gogebic Range made up for the rather docile behavior of its cross-river twin. While Hurley is certainly not within Michigan's geographical boundaries, the Montreal, Cary, Windsor, Germania, and Minnewawa Mines and the men employed therein made Hurley an interesting part of the story of the Finns in Michigan.

For whatever reason, Ironwood as a community could not keep up with Hurley's wild, audacious ways, but Annie and Leon Anderson, owners of Santini's Bar in Hurley, did recollect that folks from Ironwood would venture over the river to Hurley nightly. In a 1970s oral history interview Annie and Leon recounted, "Oh, Ironwood was always kind of dead."[54] As they describe it in its heyday (1900s–1930s) Hurley, a town of roughly three to four thousand, had "86 bars," or roughly one bar for every thirty-five persons. Annie and Leon remembered, "every building was lit up . . . I mean with electric lights." According to Santini's owners, there was legal gambling in the saloons with pots topping thousands of dollars and of course, Hurley had the "entertainers" so common to many mining communities. Leon estimated that in addition to the bars with dancers there were "maybe ten—twelve—fourteen" houses of prostitution on the various streets of Hurley's main entertainment district.[55] Hurley was of course a worst- or best-case scenario (depending upon your social proclivities) of the overtly energized trappings of proletarian life in Michigan's isolated mining regions.

The Finnish American Mining Company

In Michigan, most Finns were working in the mines of the Upper Peninsula. There was, however, a small group of ascending middle-class Copper Country Finns who owned a mine, though not in the United States. Along with Cornish American mining engineer John Daniell, who was president of the company, and Norwegian immigrant businessman Edward Ulseth, who was first vice-president, Copper Country Finns J. H. Jasberg (second vice-president), O. J. Larson (counsel), Henry Kitti (treasurer), Charles J. Jackola (secretary), and directors John Saari, Charles Wickstrom, John Benson, and Albert Jolin founded the Finnish American Mining Company in 1907. The intrepid venture capitalists chose to reopen a defunct mine in Finland known as the Orijärvi Mine. Orijärvi, located in southwestern Finland between Helsinki and Turku, consisted of four ore bodies with deposits of copper and zinc among other ores in smaller quantities. The investors split the administration of the company between offices in Finland and the Calumet State Bank Building, Room 5, in Red Jacket (Calumet).[56]

Mining must have been a tantalizing, even excessively tempting business prospect for these Finn businessmen. Being prominent entrepreneurs in the Upper Peninsula of Finnish background, these men would have seen the mining wealth of the Copper Country accumulate around them. Knowing they had created enough personal surplus wealth to spend making them richer like their fellow "upper crusters" in the Copper Country might have burned a hole in their collective pockets. Alas, mining is not all that it seems and there is many a slip betwixt the cup and the lip, to borrow a phrase from olden days.

The venture started well enough, but soon after, the operation ran into hard times. Mrs. Ralph Abrahamson, whose stepfather worked at the Orijärvi Mine, recalled in an oral history interview, "It was a real nice beginning, but it petered out."[57] This perhaps should not have been a shock, as this was not the first attempt to work the very small-bodied ore deposits at the Orijärvi. Various outfits had attempted to make a go of the property beginning in 1758, but seemingly never made the Orijärvi's copper and zinc ore bodies pay.[58] By 1915, the Orijärvi and its Finnish American investors were in dire straights, declaring bankruptcy and scampering, unsuccessfully, to pay off debts. Daniell and his Daniell Investment Company parted ways with the venture capitalist Finns before bankruptcy, possibly because he recognized the warning signs as early as 1912. Even at this stage the venture was failing to pay its debts to its own president, as a letter from Jasberg to Daniell showed: "In reply to your enquiry [sic] asking for the amount of salary due you to date from the Calumet office of the Finnish American Mining Co. (I) would say that my records show that no money has been paid to you since Sept. 30, 1911 and that there is now due to you salary for 11 months and 10 days."[59]

Things only got worse for the company and its prominent Finn businessmen. Jackola, perhaps grasping the gravity of the situation as a justice of the peace in Calumet, grew very upset when the Finnish language newspaper *Päivälehti* ran a story that was critical of the Finnish American Mining Company and its investors. Jackola was so bereft he wrote Jasberg on June 25, 1915:

> I presume that you have read in the Wednesday's issue of the *Päivälehti,* bearing date June 23, 1915, on page four under headlines "Last Chapter," the libelous article which appeared in that paper on the editorial page. . . . Inasmuch as this article reflects not only upon your personal honor and character as a citizen and fellow countrymen, but also upon all of the former directors of the Finnish American Mining Company, it is high time for all of us either jointly or personally to ask that a retraction of this article be made by this paper and its editorial staff.
>
> . . . it would appear from the contents of it [*Siirtolainen*—another paper critical of the Finnish American Mining Company] that we are all rascals, swindlers, embezzlers and crooks of the first water. I do not know whether you feel like taking any of this "dope." I believe you will not, because it was simply a speculative enterprise of which there are thousands in America and elsewhere. The old directors have taken the burden of saving the property and have taken the burden of debt upon themselves. I know that I have personally lost considerable cash and have always been ready to help the concern along as much as my means and ability have warranted.[60]

Even though the mining operation was over for the Finns, the payment for playing the always-dicey mining game was certainly not. Shortly after the Finn entrepreneurs in Michigan had their company ashamedly put on the market in a bankruptcy sale, their cohorts in Finland bought and reorganized the company, naming it the *Osakeyhtio Vuorikaivos* (Mountain Mine Stock Company). The debts incurred from the loaned capitalization of the defunct company did not, however, go away. Paying the loans or "bank notes" owed to both the Superior National Bank in Hancock and the Merchants and Miners Bank in Calumet became a dilemma of the first order. Some of the Finn investors in the Copper Country tried to ignore their debts, as a letter from the Superior National Bank to J. H. Jasberg related: "Your note for eight hundred dollars and twenty-eight dollars interest was due in this bank on Sept. 1st. We have carried this item for some time and must insist that it be paid or at least substantially reduced."[61] This letter was one of a substantial volley to collect money due to the banks from former Finnish American Mining Company investors.

As the teens turned into the 1920s, the former Finnish American Mining Company investors became successful in other areas. Jackola became vice-consul to Finland in Calumet, O. J. Larson became a congressman to the United States' House of Representatives, and Jasberg became a powerful land agent. While these seemingly respected men and leaders of the "reputable segments" of the Finnish American community enjoyed the life of the upper middle class, at the same time they were at each other's throats over financial matters. It was almost a financial war of will and words between the privileged within Finnish America. Condescending letters were sent back and forth asking for money, telegrams between the men described why there was no money to spare toward the debt, and still many more letters laid culpability on various doors.

For his part, it seemed that Jackola led the effort to remain faithful to his financial obligations. Jasberg, Larson, and Saari seemed to be the worst offenders in attempted side stepping of the debt. A 1921 letter from Jackola to Jasberg indicated that Jackola had paid $1,943.51 of the debt, Ulseth had paid $1,895.87, Daniell had paid $1,695.54, Saari had paid $530.12, Larson had paid $356.96, and Jasberg had paid only $222.17.[62] On March 25, 1925, Jackola died, but the creditors did not give up on collecting his share of the debt, his family bore that burden. The other wayward investors in the Finnish

Workers pose for photograph at a Jacobsville, Michigan, sandstone quarry, ca. 1900. Courtesy of Finlandia University's Finnish American Historical Archive, Historic Photograph Collection.

American Mining Company struggled to pay off their debts as well, but never fully recovered financially from a good prospect turned bad.

Quarry Work

At Jacobsville, Michigan, was a predominantly Finnish immigrant trade. The beautiful red, red and white, or creamy white sandstone that adorns many of the buildings throughout the Upper Peninsula mining boomtown communities came from Jacobsville, located on the eastern periphery of the Copper Country, and thus Finn quarry workers. Finns began working in the Jacobsville quarries in the mid-1880s and continued cutting the massive sandstone squares in the eastern entry of Portage Lake until brick replaced sandstone as a the preferred building material in the Upper Peninsula.[63]

Finn men drilled holes and detached the beautiful sedimentary rock from its earthen base daily in five fully operating quarries. Work in the quarries was no less toilsome than in the Copper Country's mines, and the quarried product was seemingly just as popular as Michigan copper. As Holmio wrote:

> Horses were used to move the heavy stones, some weighing tens of tons, to dock, from which they were lifted by man-and horse-powered winches to large barges. Tugs towed the barges to Chicago, Detroit and other destinations, wherever the demand was most urgent. Jacobsville sandstone was used as far away as New York, where the Waldorf-Astoria Hotel was built with Jacobsville sandstone. The industry was at its peak between 1890 and 1910, at which time the population of the village rose to 750 persons.[64]

Jacobsville, like many of its copper mining cohorts, developed a bustling little industrial community. Saloons and the complementary temperance society, stores and barbershops, a school, a community band, and Finnish-language Lutheran churches all bequeathed a Finnish immigrant culture in Jacobsville.[65]

Logging

Unlike with mine work, Finnish immigrant workers came to Michigan fully familiar with the work and life of a logger. Their experience with logging in Finland did not, however, mean that the work was safe or easy or on the grand scale of Michigan's timber industry. If mine work in Michigan could be described as dangerous, and if the copper and iron mining regions could be described as isolated, life for the Finnish immigrant workers in Michigan's logging industry, with its small, sparsely dotted logging camps, could be described as downright perilous and inaccessible.

Logging and logging injuries were so dangerous because workers were literally at times in the middle of nowhere, and as we hear stories about logging camp cooks and logging camp lice, we never hear of logging camp doctors. Some larger logging companies at developed industrial sites—such as Ford's logging community, Alberta, just south of L'Anse, Michigan—may have employed doctors to look after injured workers, but the many smaller, mid-sized, and large slipshod operations did not have the money or the desire to employ a doctor in the middle of the vast stands of white pine.

Scholarly and statistical analyses of worker casualties in the logging industry are for the most part difficult to come by, because there were just as many
small operations employing ten to fifteen men as there were large operations
employing seventy to eighty men. Oftentimes the camps were so isolated and
haphazardly located throughout the Upper and Lower Peninsulas that there
was no way to obtain accurate statistical figures about life in logging camps.
So, for the most part, our analysis of Finnish work in Michigan's forests will
depend on oral histories from the men who worked in the industry.

Some of the first Finns in Michigan were loggers in the Lower Peninsula.
By the 1870s, Finns were coming from the Old Country to work in the standing pine forests of the Lower Peninsula in areas around East Tawas and
Oscoda. By 1880, there were Finns working in the logging camps and mills
of Muskegon, Ludington, White Cloud, and Howard City. As the mighty
stands of white pine in the Lower Peninsula fell to the axes of the timbermen, the loggers moved on, venturing into the southeastern Upper Peninsula, northeastern Wisconsin, and the southwestern Upper Peninsula. As a
rule, because of its short-term depletive nature, logging was a transient job,
lending itself to a young, mobile workforce. Once a stand of trees was cut,
there was no choice for a logger other than to move on in search of the next
stand. Some loggers settled cutover lands and farmed, but if logging was in
the veins, putting down roots was not an option.[66]

Logging camps, like loggers, were transient or temporary outfits. They
were built rapidly and, after service, left to rot or disassembled quickly. In a
1974 oral history interview, sawmill owner Reuben Niemisto of Pelkie, Michigan, described the buildings in Matt Oja's logging camp circa 1930:

Well, what they used to, first of all you had a have a cook camp, you know
that was a building in itself where the cook used to have these long tables
. . . three rows, and it was a long building, I would say about 20–25 feet wide
and quite long, maybe sixty feet long and made out of rough lumber, just tar
paper on the outside and of course the cook, he lived there in a little nook
in the corner . . . and they then also had what they called sleeping quarters
for the men's quarters which was another building. And they had double
bunks on both sides and . . . a great big stove in about the middle of the thing
(building) . . . yeah and they hung their socks to dry after work. Wooden
floors, of course, and they had of course a big horse barn. At that time they

Hauling logs by sleigh in winter, Askel Hill, Michigan, ca. 1925. Courtesy of Finlandia University's Finnish American Historical Archive, Hanka Homestead Collection.

were still dragging the logs out with horses . . . then they had a blacksmith shop . . . they had a office with a clerk.[67]

As previously stated, logging was a very dangerous occupation. Sawyers, those who cut trees, had to watch for widow makers and falling timber, which was dangerous, but another job in the industry was perhaps even more dangerous. After sawyers cut logs in winter, a driver or teamster and a team of horses would pull or "skid" logs close to a river, waiting for spring thaw. In the spring, the logs were pushed or dumped into the river and ridden, hundreds, thousands at a time, to a waiting mill . . . yes, men got on logs and rode them down a river. As Arthur R. Erickson, logging historian, describes:

Some of the guys were catty enough they could jump on a log and they could go right across the river like a squirrel on a log. . . . Oh, were they ever good with the canthook (an implement used for rolling or directing logs) . . . many a time I'd see them come and ride, two guys riding a log standing on that just like a bird riding along . . . boy, that was something to watch . . . they called them riverhogs at that time . . . that was wonderful to watch.[68]

Inevitably, some riverhogs departed this life through a cold, watery death, caught underneath a flowing mass of logs. Often, logs got jammed on an obstacle or narrow section in a river. To break the jam, Erickson recalled, "Yes, yes, they put in maybe a dozen sticks of dynamite, you know, right where they figure the key log was . . . big geyser of water would come up and logs and all and they'd s start to go again."[69]

Loggers received little pay for long hours. According to Erickson, "as a rule most of the guys worked for $1 a day and board [circa 1918]. . . . There was no 8-hour days then [or overtime pay]; it was from daylight till dark."[70] Towns close to logging camps catered to the young men coming out of the woods. Erickson recalls that in Baraga, Michigan, "it seemed that almost every other building was a saloon."[71] When young men who had been isolated for months on end hit a town, in most instances it took much longer for the town to recover than it did for the hung-over men. Annie and Leon Anderson of Santini's Bar in Hurley recalled, "they [the loggers] spent . . . if they had a dollar everybody drank. They stayed in the woods for about three or four months and got their pay and then they'd all come in and they wouldn't leave until the money was all gone."[72]

Loggers were a colorful lot. They were generally a hardworking, hard drinking, and hard living bunch throughout the Upper Peninsula, but perhaps nowhere more so than in the eastern Upper Peninsula outpost of Seney. According to Holmio:

. . . there were many Finnish loggers and wood cutters in Seney. Up to the present time, no records have been found of their intellectual interests. They built neither churches nor temperance halls, nor did ministers apparently ever stop there to preach. The Finns, along with those of other nationalities, sank into the corruption and wildness of logging camp life. An incident that occurred in the very first days of the village's existence gave a glimpse of what was to come. When the first trainload of lumberjacks arrived from southern Michigan, they kicked in and smashed all the windows of the train to show what life there was going to be like.

There are many other stories—almost legends—about Finns here, as elsewhere, especially about their drinking, physical strength, and fighting ability when thoroughly aroused:

One Saturday evening a Finnish woodcutter went into a saloon and ordered drinks. When he paid for them, the others saw his bundle of bills. When he left the place a non-Finn started after him. The saloonkeeper warned him, "Don't follow him, he's a Finn!" But the other paid no heed. Half an hour later there was a weak knock at the saloon door, and in crawled the would-be thief covered with blood. The Finn had had pity on his assailant and had spared his life, but to remind him of the transitoriness of life, he had given him dozens of small knife wounds.[73]

Unfortunately, Holmio does not reference this source, so we have no way of knowing if it is embellished, but the take-away message of the preceding story is that logging camps and loggers had colorful but very difficult lives. Holmio's blatant romanticism of the Finn logger and logging camp life is regrettable. As further evidence of some shortcomings in his otherwise well-documented research, a page later Holmio writes, "Whenever a socialist agitator appeared at a logging camp, he usually left in a hurry, for everyone appeared to be satisfied with conditions as they were. The owners and managers of lumber camps made money, and the workmen had good times, in keeping with their small requirements."[74]

This is false. George Rahkonen, Finnish American and former secretary/treasurer of Michigan's Timberworker's Union, recounted the efforts to organize Michigan timber workers in the Upper Peninsula. With help from a Minnesota timber workers' American Federation of Labor local, a 1937 meeting in Ironwood called for local loggers and sawmill operators to apply for a charter from the AFL's Carpenters and Joiners for a Lumber and Sawmill Workers' local.[75] The charter was granted on March 14, 1937, and Local 2530 set about combating the ills of the logging industry, because, as George recalled:

The conditions of the timber workers had changed little since the beginning of logging. No state laws regulating camp construction, housing of workers in camps or health or sanitary conditions existed. Many of the camps were mere hovels with no bathing or washing facilities. Men slept in wooden bunks on straw-filled mattresses. Unwashed blankets became infested with ticks and lice. Food was stored in unscreened areas, overrun with flies and rodents. Men worked 9–10 hour days at the rate of 27 to 30 cents an hour for unskilled labor and slightly higher for skilled labor. From this, 80 cents to a dollar a day was deducted for board. The industrial accident rate was high, comparable to that of mining.[76]

By 1937, a number of Michigan loggers had had enough in their dealings with medium to large timber companies, and the conditions in the woods brought things to loggerheads. An organizer for the union went to Ironwood and then on to Marenisco, Michigan. While the organizer was in Marenisco, the Bonifas Mill fired a Finn logger by the name of John Maki for advocating unionism. With Maki's firing, the union organizer had a cause and rallied fellow workers around it; a strike was called on May 19, 1937. After looking for several leaders, the union looked to Rahkonen to represent workers in the dispute. As he entered Marenisco to sign up workers to enlarge the number of strikers, he found the streets filled with striking loggers. Rahkonen set up a sign-in station at a local saloon and began administrating the strike, even though he had never worked a day in the woods.

Organizational help was soon to arrive and Finnish American presence in the strike was significant as Matt Savola, an experienced mine union organizer who was at that time working in the woods around Iron River, came to Marenisco along with Frank Walli, a former organizer for the National Mine Workers Union, and John Wiita, a district organizer for the Communist Party. According to Rahkonen, within a few weeks all the camps in Gogebic County were out on strike. The strike was well organized, with offices in Ironwood, North Ironwood, and Bessemer pumping out strike bulletins, newspaper releases, and appeals for support and donations. A strike committee of forty persons convened to organize workers across the Upper Peninsula. In time, according to Rahkonen, an estimated six thousand Michigan timber workers were carrying union cards.[77]

The success of the union's actions incited the logging companies' owners to set about combating the union's influence. Sensing problems, Michigan governor Frank Murphy sent Harold Ashmore from the Department of Labor to arbitrate the strike. Ashmore's work was for naught. After logging company owners refused collective bargaining at the first arbitration meeting in Newberry, the union walked out of the meetings. After this walkout in Newberry, things got nasty. Rahkonen cited a National Labor Relations Board report when he wrote, "John Kist, one of a delegation of 100 unarmed strikers who marched on the Newberry Lumber and Chemical Plant the morning of June 4, was brutally attacked and clubbed to death by plant officials. The Luce County coroner listed Kist's death as follows: 'died from natural causes and overexertion.'"[78]

Rahkonen recollected that the *Ontonagon Miner,* a small newspaper serving Ontonagon County, Michigan, advocated using the "Newberry Solution" to end the strike. Violence erupted across the Upper Peninsula and, according to Rahkonen, violence against the strikers specifically increased. Dynamite was tossed at a striker's camp in Green, a bullet shattered the front window of August Heino's car in the Covington-Amasa area, and union offices in Ironwood, North Ironwood, and Bessemer were vandalized, culminating in the kidnapping and beating of three union office workers. Purportedly, violence from the union side occurred when Ero Maki, a union supporter from L'Anse, dynamited a bridge. Rahkonen writes that Maki got ten to twenty years for the crime, while not a single vigilante was arrested. However, Governor Murphy later pardoned Maki.[79]

After a plea from the governor of Minnesota, among others, Governor Murphy set up a commission to look at vigilante violence and bring the two sides back to the bargaining table. Workers and medium-sized companies agreed to terms, but the larger outfits did not budge. After sixteen weeks, workers voted to go back to work, but voted to go back as an organized body with grievance committees to bring up concerns with logging companies. Organized labor had made significant inroads into the deep white pine forests of the Upper Peninsula.[80]

Rahkonen's account of the strike was one side of a significant story. Folks on the other side of the dialectic most likely had a different view, but as Rahkonen concludes, the 1937 strike had far-reaching implications for Michigan's timber workers: " . . . it was one of the most beautiful things I've ever seen. That comes about when a group of people, one of the lowest classes of people on the totem pole of laborers, begin to express their desires and do something."[81]

Factories

As farms began to fall short and when Hank Ford introduced his $5 day, a
giant sucking sound could be heard pulling people from the industrial areas
of the Upper Peninsula into Detroit. This southward migration affected the
Finns in Michigan as well. To be sure, there were Finns in the Detroit area
long before the coming of the automobile age. Perhaps some came in the
1850s and 1860s as seamen and were later followed by businessmen and
laborers in the Detroit area salt mines between 1880 and 1905, but when the
assembly line started pumping out cars, the pull of guaranteed labor and better wages lured many Finns from the small country hamlets, logging sidings,
and mining communities of the Upper Peninsula.[82]

Though the numbers of Finns in Detroit was never the same as those in
the Upper Peninsula, they were a very distinct ethnic group in the peopling of
that mighty industrial city and their numbers increased in Detroit in a short
time. In 1900, there were 4 Finns living in all of Wayne County (home county
of the Detroit metropolitan area). In 1910, there were 59 Finns in Detroit.
By 1930, there were 2,811. The growth of the Finnish population in Detroit
mirrored the overall increase in Detroit's population and significance to industrial America. In 1904, during the initial stage of the automobile industry,
there were 50,000 workers on automobile company payrolls. This number
skyrocketed to 170,000 by 1919. Detroit's population mimicked this trend. In
1900, there were less than 300,000 people in Detroit, but by 1930, there were
a million and a half. Joining the Finns were southeastern Europeans, Poles,
Germans, Scandinavians, and yes, even Canadians.[83]

Into this great industrial salad bowl entered Finns from small agricultural
hamlets dotted across the Upper Peninsula. For many Finns it was the first
time they had seen an African-American, another group that was teeming
into Detroit at around the same time. Unlike in many areas of the Upper Peninsula, almost all Detroit Finns had lived somewhere else in the United States
before coming to the city.[84] For these Finns fresh off the rutabaga truck from
the northerly wilds of the Upper Peninsula, it must have been culture shock
all over again. For many Finnish immigrants who first came to the Upper
Peninsula, its mines and cities, with their comparatively fast living, were one
thing, but Detroit was a whole different ballgame. Certainly, Calumet, Ishpeming, Negaunee, Marquette, Ironwood, and Hurley had their fancy stores

and all-night saloons, but the commercial areas of many of these mining boomtown cities spanned only a couple of streets and then residential areas slowly tapered off into wilderness or vast industrialized treeless landscapes. In Detroit, on the other hand, the urban taper never seemed to come.

As in many of the other landscapes in Michigan, Finns adapted to the Detroit urban milieu, but became a definite out-group. As Holmio wrote, "Because the thousands of Finns who first came to Detroit had either been born in Finland and had lived in the Upper Peninsula for some time or were the children of Finnish born citizens, they were recognized by their Finnish accent and by the outspokenness of the miners. They often heard themselves called, 'Northern Hillbillies'"[85]

Finns quickly set up distinctive ethnic enclaves in the city, and Finn organizations followed. The labor groups were the first to organize, doing so in 1906, and by 1920 they had organized a summer camp at Loon Lake; later followed religious groups and in 1940 a nationalist group called the Knights and Ladies of Kaleva.[86] The out-migration from areas of the Upper Peninsula added greatly to southeastern Michigan's future population. Holmio tallied that by 1960, there were 40,000 persons of Finnish descent in southeastern Michigan's greater metropolitan areas.[87] The Finnish Center Association, established in 1966 in Farmington Hills, Michigan,[88] is a tangible representation of this fruitful peopling of southeastern Michigan's urban centers and resulting movement away from the Upper Peninsula's rural hamlets.

Michael Loukinen, a Finnish American sociologist at Northern Michigan University, tracked the experiences of migrant Finn workers from Pelkie, a small rural hamlet in Upper Michigan, to and within Detroit. If we consider Pelkie a typical rural hamlet, then Loukinen's research answers the question as to what precipitated the decline of many immigrant Finn agricultural settlements in the Upper Peninsula. Loukinen wrote, "The Finnish immigrant pioneers who married and settled in Pelkie raised an average of 6.5 children per family that survived to young adulthood. Out of every four children, three left their rural communities. Fifty-nine percent of all of the second generation Finnish-American children (in Pelkie) migrated to Detroit."[89] This movement began before 1920 and picked up steam, even through the Great Depression.[90]

The outflow continued into the War World II era, but reduced after 1945. When reason for migrating is given, the main explanation is economic, much as in the initial immigration of Finns into America. Many of the folks in this second-generation migration from Pelkie to Detroit worked in the industries and trades that were booming around the success of the automobile industry. For some, just getting off the farm was a major attraction, as one woman in the study described: "I did not want to stay on the farm! I wanted to get as far away from it as I could. Milking cows, getting water, spreading hay and straw, and shoveling cow shit . . . I did not like that at all."[91]

A remarkable point in Loukinen's study was that women, more so than men, headed for the bright lights and big city living of Detroit. This was especially true during the war eras.[92] America's industrial plants and factories became deceptively egalitarian in times of war. For many women, Detroit and the fast-paced assembly line lifestyle offered economic independence, social freedom, and a nonagrarian challenge that was much different from the more traditional, low-paying, labor-intensive occupations of Finnish immigrant women in America.

Finns at Work in Michigan: Traditional Labor

ining, logging, and factory work were certainly three large sources of employment for the Finns in Michigan, but other jobs also held important status in their work-a-day world. This chapter will examine work that was more familiar to Finns from experiences in the Old Country. In the jobs highlighted in this chapter, we also find the preeminence of one of the most important laborers in the Finnish immigrant community in Michigan, the female worker. Women provided labor that drove most families and supported many Finnish immigrant and American communities.

This chapter also chronicles one of the most cherished of all Finnish immigrant jobs, farming. Many Finn immigrants in Michigan identified themselves as agriculturalists. They may have worked in a mine, but they were in mining only as long as it took to save up money to buy land they could call their own. Farms were the preferred means of labor, but Finn farms offered many difficult obstacles. The "stump farms" of many Finnish immigrant families were often littered with huge white-pine stumps or marshy, mosquito-infested swamplands. As part of what can only be termed subsistence agriculture, many individuals and families labored in subsidiary "occupations" such as domestic servants, berry picking, commercial fishing, and/or hunting and trapping to supplement the agricultural lifestyle. Subsistence life and all of its trappings was for many Finns who chose this laboring life a worthwhile, though incredibly difficult, existence.

Farming

As logging outfits left vast tracts of land treeless, stump-laden landscapes, and when Finn miners left industrial areas during strikes or after mine accidents, Finns migrated back to the land to pursue what was for many their first love, farming. For most Finnish immigrants, mining was not the end game. The agricultural life, where they could be their own boss, set their own hours, and live by the rhythms of the natural world, was idyllic. By 1920, there were 30,096 Finns in Michigan and some 85 rural communities settled on the margins of industrial Michigan.[93] In the Copper Country, places like Tapiola, Elo, Pelkie, Toivola, Heinola, Oskar Bay, Salo, Wasa, and Oneco served as oases from the deafening thud and clang of industrial machinery. In southern sections of the Copper Country, Wainola and Wasas beckoned many discontent industrial Finns to the countryside. North Hurley and Little Girl's Point provided Finns refuge from industrial life on the Gogebic Range. Places like Bruce's Crossing, Trenary, Eben Junction, Chatham, Rock, and Kiva drew from the Marquette, Menominee, and Copper Country ranges. These well though sparsely popu-lated agricultural areas were places where Finns found two cherished things: land and a lifestyle they could call their own.

Typical of Finns on Michigan's industrial peripheries is the ethnic agricul-tural settlement of Aura, Michigan. Almost opposite Houghton and Hancock across Keweenaw Bay, Aura may as well have been in Finland, for it bore no resemblance to the ever-so-close Copper Country. There were no mines, no copper ore mills, and no smelters. The only industry, the transient logging industry, had come and gone, leaving a barren landscape, attractive perhaps only to Finns who were determined to live outside the copper industry's milieu. In her book about the Aura community, Elsie Collins summarized reasons for seeking the agricultural life in Aura:

> Andrew Lehto . . . succeeded in transferring his family to Pointe Abbaye
> (north of Aura); but in the fall of 1915 he returned to mine employment and
> was crushed to death in the Phoenix Mine when three tons of rock fell on
> him. Another reason for the Finns' discontent in the Copper Country was

the refusal by the Calumet and Hecla Mining Company to sell them land to build their homes or to develop their farms. Land was available only on lease; a condition that violated the Finns' long cherished dream of private ownership of the land they tilled.

Finally, after the controversial strike of 1913-14 . . . the future settlers of Aura were moved to risk one more venture toward their independence. Somewhere in America, they said, there must be a quiet spot. . . . In such a place, on their own land, they could live honorably, judging and being judged by one standard only: how hard are you willing to work.[94]

Aura's first settlers, the Hiltunen family, were typical of this latter example. In the early 1910s, Tobias Hiltunen, frustrated with working conditions and wages in the Copper Country, moved from mining community to community. When a recently arrived immigrant friend died in a mining accident, Hiltunen gladly joined the ranks of the union in the 1913-14 strike. Tobias walked the picket lines and made skis while waiting out the strike. In the midst of the strike, Tobias heard of cutover land for sale by the Hebard Lumber Company at a place known as Pointe Abbaye. Tobias and family sold some household furniture, loaded the rest on a rail car, and headed for Hebard's abandoned Mining Camp #3. Hebard Logging Company left the camp's office standing to use as a residence for the Hiltunen family, and thus the migration from industrial community to Aura "stump farm" began as refugee Finn industrial families made a life amid the barren, stump-laden landscape.[95]

Strikes did not always precipitate migration to the industrial periphery. Finnish migration to rural, logged out areas of Michigan began in the Lower Peninsula as early as the 1870s and 1880s in areas around Grayling, Jennings, and Lake City.[96] Early areas of Finn agricultural settlement appeared almost as soon as Finns entered Michigan's Upper Peninsula, and places like Askel, Tapiola, and Bruce's Crossing sprang out of the Upper Peninsula forests in the early to mid-1890s. Cutover timberlands in the Upper Peninsula were cheap; just before World War I a forty-acre tract of land cost $400-500 in what is now Rock, Michigan.[97] Land acquired through the Homestead Act was even cheaper at $1.25 per acre, but had to be cleared at the rate of an acre per year to maintain homestead rights.

Agricultural operations in the acidic, shallow soils and short growing seasons of Michigan's Upper Peninsula were subsistence operations at best, and often subsistence was difficult. Finn subsistence farms were mostly dairy operations supplemented with butchering (hogs and chickens, typically), hunting, fishing, gathering, and trapping activities. In addition to animal husbandry, Finn farmers cultivated hay or grain crops for animal feed and human utilization (typical grains grown were rye, oats, and autumn wheat), grew root crops (potatoes and rutabagas), and maintained apple orchards or other semi-domesticated berries.

Up to this point, we have tread lightly over a huge segment of Finns in the "Finns at Work in Michigan," namely Finn immigrant women. This was done somewhat purposefully because it was most often men, and mostly young men, that streamed into Michigan's industrial centers during early periods of immigration. Farms and homesteads, however, were a place where women joined alongside men in laboring. A very old Finnish saying is that if the Finn man was the head of the household, the Finn woman was the neck that turned the head; this was likely more true on farms than anywhere else in Finnish America.[98]

For the Victorian era, this was unusual. The "upper crusters" of the time might have scoffed, "How dare a woman work alongside or share the same status as a man?" but this was the status quo and not the progressive exception on Finnish farms. Women raked hay, butchered small animals, tended gardens, milked and herded cows, and took over the managerial duties of the farm when the patriarch was gone for extended stays in other employment or, in worst-case scenarios, due to abandonment or death.[99]

Physical structures on Finn farmsteads in Michigan were frequently driven by *function* over *form* and often consisted of wonderfully ramshackle collections of hand-hewed log and rough-sawn wood-framed, tarpaper-covered buildings. Finns often arranged their farmsteads in an open court-yard pattern, reminiscent of local areas in Finland. Kaups and others have demonstrated that Finn farmsteads in America are adaptations to the local environment as well as extensions of local Finnish folk traditions. Ann Marin borrows from Kaups's identification of the typical cultural characteristics of Finn farmsteads in America, which includes eight items:

> The *lato*, or field barn; the connecting barn constructed in different stages; multiple roof line of structures; log structures of squared timbers; the

Women raking hay on a Heinola, Michigan, farm, ca. 1915. Courtesy of Finlandia University's Finnish American Historical Archive, Libby Koski-Bjorklund Photograph Collection.

presence of ladders along the sides of roofs of buildings; a larger percentage of unpainted structures; the covered stoop and the rural roadside garage.[100]

People often associate innumerable outbuildings with Finn farmsteads in America, but this is not necessarily correct. Marin utilized geographer Eugene Van Cleef's tabulations, which record that, on average, Finn farmsteads had 7.2 buildings, while farmsteads of other nationalities had 6.2 buildings.[101] Typical buildings on a Finn farmstead at the turn of the century were a house, a cattle barn with a hay mow, a main hay barn, a horse barn, a chicken coop, a tool shed, an outhouse, and of course the sauna.

A quick note about the buildings: saunas were essential to the farmstead and typically one of the first or the first building erected. Due to the heat source, families could live in the sauna while other buildings were being erected, and frankly, saunas were so important to the social and cultural life that they were obligatory buildings on any farm. The cow barn complex on Finn farmsteads often had a "dogtrot" breezeway because the buildings in

the barn complex were often constructed at different periods and then con-
nected with a single roof, creating the breezeway. This design enabled a hay
cart to pull into the breezeway and unloaded into the haymow or main hay
barn that sat to the side of the cow barn. The outhouse was typically grafted
onto the back of the barn complex.[102]

Other buildings found on Finn farmsteads were artisan shops, such as a
blacksmith shop, a *riihi* or grain-drying building, a grain storage shed, sheep
and pig barns, a milk house, root cellars (often two; one cellar for root crops
and another for apples), and "satellite" hay barns. Satellite hay barns are an
interesting feature of Finn farmsteads. Some landscape historians conclude
that satellite hay barns were a laborsaving device. Many Finn farmsteads
sat on undulating hill lands, interspersed with swampy bottomlands and
marshes. One theory hypothesizes that satellite hay barns were utilized to
store hay or grain until winter, when transporting the amassed crop would
be easier over frozen, lined tracks in the snow.[103] An alternate explanation
is that satellite barns hedged the bets on the annual hay crop. Hay crops
and thus hay barns were notorious for catching on fire, and perhaps satellite
barns were used as a type of insurance, holding reserves of hay in an auxiliary
building in case of fire in the main hay barn.

A trend very typical in Finn subsistence agriculture was development of
seasonal work strategies. A seasonal work strategy enabled Finn agricultural
families to cope with the rigors of subsistence farming. Often this meant
farming in the late spring, summer, and early fall and then switching to wage
work such as mining or logging in the winter. As Marin wrote, "[the Finn
farmer] utilized his farm and home expertise to meet material needs when
money was not available. However, money was necessary for supplies, taxes
and debts. Rarely was income from the selling of products such as potatoes
and cream sufficient. A supplementary income was a necessity. Often the
Finns earned this by selling pulpwood and railroad ties or by working in
mines or lumber camps for several months each year."[104]

Agriculture was so important to one Finn Upper Peninsula community
that a school was devoted to its development. The Doelle School, or Otter
Lake Agricultural School, located in Tapiola, was the first "Ag" school in
Michigan. Founded in 1913 by legislation of Michigan's state government,
the Doelle was home to "six rooms, consisting of classrooms, laboratory,
kitchen, and manual training department, [which] not only serves as a

Hanka Homestead

An outstanding extant example of the Finnish immigrant homestead in America is the Hanka Homestead in Askel, Michigan. The homestead, restored to circa 1920, has nine buildings situated at their original locations within the farmstead. The historic integrity of the farm is very high and acknowledged by the federal government as a listing on the National Register of Historic Places, 1984. As much as possible, original materials, at times scavenged from the woods, were used to reconstruct buildings that had deteriorated over time. The historic landscape also has very high integrity. A line strung to deliver telephone service, in one of the first rural phone services in the Keweenaw, is extant, as well as the fields and apple trees that were such an important part of the farmstead's sustainability. Perhaps the most important visitor experience at the farm is the immediate sense of isolation and self-sufficiency needed by Finnish immigrant homesteaders.

Highlights of the farm are the *savu* sauna, joker (parted-out farm utility vehicle), blacksmith shop, farmhouse, and hand-dug and rock-lined cistern well with fulcrum-lever bucket system. The *savu*, or smoke sauna, has interesting features and its blackened timbers well relate the efforts taken to ensure that original materials were used in the reconstruction of the building. It is probably the most venerated building, and for good reason. *Savu* saunas were essential components in almost every early Finn farmstead. In them Finns smoked meat and/or fish, dried leaves and bark, distilled liquor, washed clothes, dried and shelled peas and beans, malted wheat, dried grain, made candles, practiced cupping and massage, and delivered children. The sauna is often described as a building that is integral to all phases of life, because Finns used it to begin life, to end life, and for everything in-between. Hanka Homestead is open for guided tours during the summer months.

school house, but is a community center around which the life of the district revolves. In connection with the school there is a farm of forty acres where crops are grown (including tobacco), pure-blooded stock raised and tests of soil."[105] The community dedicated a second Doelle School in 1931 after the first school succumbed to a fire in 1929.

The second Doelle building exists to this day in Tapiola, but it is in rough condition. Like many of the Finn farming communities that existed on the industrial periphery of Michigan's boom time mining operations, the Doelle has fallen into disrepair. Yet, the Doelle silently endures the ravages of time along with an adjacent field surrounded by a school-sponsored red pine plantation seeded in 1940. These two iconographic features remain as a testament to the labor of Finns in all agricultural communities on Michigan's industrial peripheries.[106]

Domestics and Boarding House Operators

The number one occupation of females in the Finnish immigrant population was domestic servant. Often domestics or "maids" as they were more commonly known, were young women "fresh off the boat" from Finland and very much the cohort of the thousands of young Finnish immigrant men that streamed into Michigan. Though female domestics did not face the dangers inherent in mining, they did face the prevailing prejudiced and segregated Victorian social setting that laboring Finn men faced both above and below ground.

This Victorian social scene dictated a strong class division between servant and "served." Finn maids were good enough to work in rich folks' homes, but not good enough to have dinner there, or in many instances, live in the same community. As a representative tangible element of the Victorian distinction in social status between classes, physical space often set off boss from worker. Laurium, Michigan, an elite bedroom community of Red Jacket (Calumet), Michigan, was home to many of the well-to-do officials of the Calumet area mines, as well as many of the entrepreneurs and professionals of that copper mining kingdom. Many of the maids that served the quasi-aristocrats of Laurium lived in Tamarack Location, a drab mining town consisting of cookie-cutter houses regimented in monotonous rows. Domestic servants worked long hours, perhaps even longer than their male counterparts in the area mines, likely for less money. Servants received only one day off. In Laurium that day was Thursday and was known in that community as "Maid's Day Off."[107]

Though most domestic servants were young women, often older, widowed women had to revert to a job designed for youthful hands and backs.

Josephine Makela faced some of the typical problems of Finn women in the Upper Peninsula's remote industrial frontier when her husband died of a suspicious heart attack in one of Neguanee's iron mines. She had children to feed and clothe, had to pay rent, and had to act as both a father and a mother to her growing kids. In a time before the full recognition of labor and social reforms of the Progressive Era, Josephine and her six children had no such thing as social security or workers' compensation to fall back on; Josephine had to become a domestic. As her daughter Sandra Sarkela remembers:

> . . . and then she started working for people by the day, you know, to do house cleaning and washing for people. But even by 1920, those people that she went to wash for and they were well-to-do people, they did not have any electric washers. She had to do all the washing by hand, even for those people. The times were really tough for her.[108]

While her husband was still alive, Josephine operated another labor-intensive, female-dominated business in Negaunee, a boarding house. Much as men employed seasonal work strategies to supplement their income, women added to their family's income by taking in boarders. As we have previously mentioned, mining and logging were very physically demanding jobs, but being a boarding house mistress was no less demanding and was perhaps even more so because the work never ended. The quitting bell rang after ten hours in the mines, but it never rang at a boarding house. There was always work to do when a woman took boarders into her home.

While running her boarding house, Josephine administered to twenty-two men, her only help being her teen-age daughter Sandra. The two intrepid women got up at four in the morning to begin preparations for the day's meals, ironing, and house cleaning. For all this, the cleaning of the miners' clothes, the making of meals including lunch buckets for the mines, and the washing of the bed linens, Josephine received $20.00 a month from each border. The Makelas also tended to four milk cows at this time right in the city limits of Negaunee, as Sandra remembers: "everybody had one or two cows, but then when my mother had so many boarders . . . she had to have four cows."[109]

Berry Picking

Berries were an important part of the Finn diet in Michigan. Along with apples and other gathered fare, berries added both supplementary nutrition and taste variance to a diet that was chocked full of the five Finn food groups: meat (salted and smoked), dairy, fish, potatoes, and rutabagas. Finns enjoyed the fruits of nature's candy shop, picking blueberries, raspberries, blackberries, thimbleberries, and strawberries. Strawberry picking was interesting, in that it attained a somewhat commercial status, especially in Chassell, Michigan, a small logging-agricultural community on the Copper Country's industrial periphery. Strawberry picking was such a cottage industry that Chassell became home to a cooperative strawberry growers association in the late 1930s and 40s.[110]

Berry picking was a time to get together with family, a sort of communal experience for all to enjoy, but for young men (pre-teen and teenagers) the berry business could be a serious endeavor. A letter from Ensio Björklund to his cousin Ruth Juntilla discussed the bountiful harvest in Oskar along the Portage Lake Canal in 1923:

> Maana (Grandma) told me to write you and tell you to come over here because there is so much strawberries to pick. She said that you (are) to come with Tikkanen as soon as you can come. We pick strawberries each day and still cannot get the strawberry fields half picked.
>
> We have sent two truckloads already to town to Lepisto's store. He is coming the third time tonight or tomorrow night to get some more. I think he is coming to get our strawberries all summer. You's do not need to take any orders there.
>
> Tell Paul [cousin] to come here to pick strawberries if he has not got any work. Tell your mother to come pick strawberries on some Sunday before they all go. We pick on Tuesday 120 quarts or about 7 cases. On Wednesday we pick 69 quarts or 4 cases and 5 quarts.
>
> P.S. Let Paul read this letter if he cares to. From mine and Paul's field I got 14 quarts of strawberries but did not get the money yet. Better come tonight if you can and Pauly too.[111]

For the most part women and children picked berries, but when there was free time from logging, mining, or other farm chores, men joined in the picking. To some extent, berry picking was tough work, and not everyone in the family cared much for the fieldwork. Evelyn Turunen remembered:

> Yes, we used to pick berries and that I do remember, I have developed a real distaste for picking berries because we used to go out and pick raspberries, at the Hazel corner (to the south and west of Pelkie, Michigan) there's a lot of berries there and that was something that we had to do . . . and then at one time, too, there were a lot of blueberries in Hazel swamp and we used to have to go there too, and it was usually an all day affair and then it wasn't bad enough picking there, but when we came back home we had to clean all those pails and pails of berries and I just never liked to pick berries ever since then.[112]

Evelyn disliked berry picking so much, she mutinied on one berry picking excursion:

> When one of my brothers was at home, I think he had been away from home and he had come back, and he had gone to pick raspberries further off because I remember we had gone with the car and I thought, well, gee, that's going to be quite an event because they sort of talked about this being a picnic . . . and we had been out there for a while and I picked for a while and I got tired of it so I went and sat in the car and he was so angry with me because I ate almost all the sandwiches . . . they really didn't think I was worth bringing along because I ate up most of the lunch.[113]

Moonshine

Often described as "white lightening in a bottle," moonshine was a precious commodity for some Finns; so much so, its production became a cottage industry of sorts. In prohibition times, whiskey was officially outlawed, but tacitly sanctioned as Vienna Laine, currently of Escanaba, remembers:

I remember going to these medicine shows where these men would be selling this elixir of life, it turned out to be whiskey of course. [People] would go there and buy it legally at fancy shows.[114]

When times got tough for folks, people made due with what they had and for some prohibition was the toughest of times. During these teetotaling times, people had a thirsty supply side itching for a bit of black market home brew. Even the most unlikely of characters joined in the distilling of whiskey. As Vienna recalls:

I had a friend who was born and raised on a farm west of Rock . . . her parents were from Finland and she had two kids . . . her husband went out cutting wood, never came back for supper. They went to look for him and found him under a tree, he had died of a heart attack. So, here's a widow who doesn't speak English with two little girls, she tried to run the farm, the younger girl was born with lupus . . .

She had a real good friend who ran a boarding house in Escanaba that was held in high esteem. The lady who ran the boarding house said to the lady that, "you're crazy to try and run that farm yourself. I could give you a little money and you could try making whisky." This is prohibition everybody made whisky, you're not going to stop Finns or Russians or anybody else from making whiskey.

They [the lady and her two daughters] had one of these tooling cars and her daughter would drive the car all over the place and once the lady had loaned her the money and taught her how to work the still, she [the lady's thirteen year-old daughter] was all over with whiskey. The grown-ups told her that nobody will suspect this thirteen-year-old girl would have a trunk full of whiskey bottles and she delivered and had a regular route . . .

They made it [the whiskey] out of corn mash, they bought sugar and stored the mash and distilled [product] in the sauna under the floor. In the main sauna room [on a makeshift cook stove] the brew was distilled from corn sugar. They used a coloring agent to make the liquid look brown.[115]

Apparently, the key was to not become too big an operation. If you went to the store and bought ten bags of corn, okay; if you bought one hundred, the local authorities knew something was up and were perhaps forced to

Women and men cleaning fish in a Lake Superior Fisheries building, Hancock, Michigan, ca. 1940. Courtesy of Finlandia University's Finnish American Historical Archive, Bea (Nurmi) Meyers Photograph Collection.

act. Whiskey making seems to have been tacitly sanctioned as long as no one got out of control with production. In many of Michigan's small Finnish agricultural communities, whiskey was used as a sort of commodity in local bartering networks. Vienna recalled that her family had moonshine around all the time, but never drank any.[116] The whiskey was used as a social lubricant, gesture of good will, and trading item in a time when money was tight, but copper tubing, raw materials, and a whole lot of ingenuity was prevalent.

Fishing

Fishing was done on a variety of scales in Michigan's vast waters. Many Finns in Michigan fished inland lakes and rivers simply as a way to supplement their subsistence diets, but for other Finns fishing was a way of life that led them to the tempestuous waters of Lake Superior, Lake Huron, or Lake Michigan. The bays and inlets of the Great Lakes were home to entire villages of people whose life revolved around the waters of the mighty lakes.

Many of the small Finn fishing villages in Michigan were collectively oriented. Many Finns trolling Michigan's waters believed that a cooperative production strategy was best for the common good of the fishermen and their families. Indicative of this was Lake Superior Fisheries, a division of Northern Cooperatives, which packaged and distributed fish in Hancock, Michigan. In the fall of 1943, Bea (Nurmi) Meyers's father took a job as manager of the Lake Superior Fisheries cooperative commercial operation.[117]

Truck drivers from Lake Superior Fisheries would travel to Skanee, Aura, Portage Entry, and Big Traverse Bay to collect catches of trout and whitefish from fishermen. Drivers then brought the catches to Hancock, where the fish were filleted, packaged, frozen, and put on ice. Lake Superior Fisheries then distributed the fish to restaurants and stores all over Michigan, Wisconsin, and Minnesota. Some trout and whitefish caught by Finn fishermen in Lake Superior's waters and packaged by Lake Superior Fisheries even made their way to Chicago on overnight trains for posh restaurants. Some of the catch then continued on from Chicago to New York City. Fresh fish was the standard. As Bea recalls, the motto for Lake Superior Fisheries was, "The fish you eat today, slept last night in Keweenaw Bay." For a time, business at the fisheries cooperative was so good that Bea herself, who worked as a bookkeeper for her father throughout high school, had to deliver fish to area restaurants in the coop's trucks.[118]

During World War II, Finn fishermen caught and Lake Superior Fisheries packaged herring for men overseas. At this time, the number of workers at the fish packing plant in Hancock swelled to over one hundred people. A group of people filleted the herring and then passed the herring on to another group that packed the small fish into forty-pound tins. The tins were then placed into the coop's–40-degree freezers within dry ice. The blocks of ice with fish frozen inside were then separated from the tins and shipped to men and women in uniform.[119] In this roundabout way, Finn fishermen and their families served the United States admirably during World War II, even though some never stepped foot out of Michigan.

Reindeer Herding

Though reindeer herding was never a large supplier of work for the Finns in Michigan, it was part of an interesting migration for several Finn-Sámi men from the Copper Country and shows the relative diversity of the Finnish immigrant population in Michigan. Finland had and still maintains a sizeable

Five of the eight Sámi reindeer herders who returned from Alaska to the Copper Country ca. 1906. Courtesy of Finlandia University's Finnish American Historical Archive, Gus Linja Collection.

Sámi population in the very northern hinterlands of the country. Historically, the Sámi traveled across national boundaries of Finland, Russia, Sweden, and Norway, following the massive herds of reindeer they tended as part of a unique nomadic lifestyle. Interspersed with other Finnish immigrants, a number of Sámi men, women, and children made their way from Finnish Lapland to Michigan between 1887 and 1890.[120]

In 1903, J. H. Jasberg, by request from Sheldon Jackson, general agent of education in Alaska for the United States Department of the Interior, recruited a group of Sámi men from north of Calumet to join Jackson's Reindeer Herding Project in Alaska. The Reindeer Herding Project had commenced in 1891 as a way to bring a sustainable food and clothing source to the extremely isolated mining camps and native villages of environs impacted by Alaska's gold rush era. After repeated attempts by the U.S. government to coerce Native Alaskans into adopting an entirely new cultural system by becoming reindeer herders, the government decided to send for folks who were familiar and culturally receptive toward herding reindeer. Sámi families were recruited from parts of northern Norway, Sweden, and Finland. As the pool of Sámi recruits began to shallow in Europe, Jackson's office contacted Jasberg and he recruited eight Sámi immigrants from the Copper Country for Jackson's Reindeer Herding Project in far-off Alaska.[121]

In 1904, after first stopping in San Francisco, the intrepid Michigan Sámi men headed for the Kuskokwim River in the northern part of Alaska to join a multiethnic assembly of reindeer herders, Native Alaskans, and U.S. bureaucrats. The men faced herding one thousand head of reindeer per person and tried to interact with other herders and supervisors that spoke in three different individual languages. As Sámi-Finn American historian Gustaf Linja wrote, "one can understand why for the first week or so the herds were moved only about 15–20 miles per day." As familiarity grew between the multiethnic herders the rate of travel increased to 40–60 miles per day. The Copper Country Sámi had some trouble adapting to the Native Alaskan diet of whale blubber, which was high in Vitamin C. Because of this oversight in diet, three of the eight men died of scurvy in Alaska and one of the men who died in winter was pulled as a frozen corpse over the ice-covered Alaskan tundra until spring, when he was shipped back to the United States. The five surviving men completed their mission in 1906 and returned to the Copper Country that same year.[122]

Cultural Organizations of the Finns in Michigan

As we have seen, the life of Finn workers in Michigan was a difficult existence. In this life were both good and bad slices. A good slice was that many Finns found work in Michigan and were able to save money, start families and homesteads, businesses, or the like, and thus add favorably to the building of Michigan and America. A disappointing equivalent to the good was that Finns certainly had their social problems while making this contribution. Work in its various forms provided the tangible resources for nourishment; cultural organizations provided the moral, spiritual, and political sustenance for many of these same folks. Drinking and the problems it engendered, such as fights, domestic violence, and general social malaise, plagued some Finns and thus the Finnish immigrant community.

From the earliest days of the Finns in Michigan, very diverse groups identified an assortment of social problems and in essence worked toward the same social objectives, elevating the moral consciousness of their members. The unique element of this is that they each had different strategies and ideologies for doing so and often fought about the best course of action to accomplish the same goal. A common quip about the Finns' proclivity toward social and cultural organizations is that if you see two or three Finns walking together they are probably going to start a cooperative, church, or union. While this idiom certainly has merit, the converse also has credibility. **57**

If you saw two or three Finns walking away from each other, it could be said that they were *splitting* from membership in a coop, church, or union.

Finns in Michigan and the United States in general were seemingly involved in a never-ending argument over the ideology, implementation, and development of cultural and social organizations. This rankling over ideology seemed to be a uniquely American phenomenon, as groups in Finland watched their wayward brothers and sisters in America argue over seemingly trivial principles.

In organizations such as the labor movement, church congregations, temperance societies, and even, yes, the "cooperative" movement there was a strange, erratic solidarity. Perhaps some of these groups sustained themselves and celebrated the constant open interpretation of doctrine and ideology, but it tore most groups apart from the inside. A flow chart of the fractioned organizations is on the following page.

Finnish immigrant organizational groups in America are fascinating because not only did they split with fervent gusto, they split into very diverse ideological factions. Finnish American organizations span a vast ideological gulf from radical union organizations, such as the Industrial Workers of the World (IWW), to pious and very conservative religious groups. Despite this vast array of ideologies, Finn immigrant groups often are pigeonholed into two categories: Red, or Labor Finns and White, or Church Finns, with Red Finns being the radical, labor, and political groups and White Finns being the opposing conservative, religious, and nationalist movements. These two "colors" have a basis, but vastly oversimplify the Finn organizational spectrum to the extent that they obscure the fascinating waxing and waning of ideologies and philosophies.

Perhaps at this point it would be good to reacquaint ourselves with the differences between radical, liberal, and conservative organizations. For the sake of brevity, we will use a very broad, oversimplified working definition when analyzing the various organizational groups of the Finns in Michigan. The broad difference between these groups was the amount of and pace of change or maintenance of status quo that defined their principles.

Radical groups called for very rapid change and a drastic overhaul of the current status quo, revolutionary transformation of society with total social upheaval. Liberal elements called for change at moderate rates and alteration of the status quo, not obliteration of the current social situation.

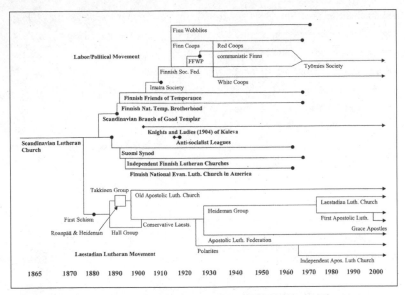

The Finnish American Organizational Family Tree in Michigan 1865–2005.

Conservative groups sought maintenance to varying degrees and continued support for the status quo. The preceding three-line breakdown seems a bit benign, and it is, but when we consider the stakeholders, social implications, and socio-economic variables, the enormity of the chasm between groups becomes apparent.

What might the Finnish Lutheran Church have to lose in a total social upheaval? What might the labor movement gain in a social upheaval? We must think about the supporting doctrine, documents, dogma, ideology, and philosophy behind each group. How do many folks feel about the Bible or about Marx's *Communist Manifesto*? Are these mere books or do they represent ways of life? These were some of the issues and reasons for clashes between Finn immigrant groups that were ostensibly working toward the same goal, getting young Finn men away from the bar and out of the newspaper headlines for fighting, providing an abode for homesick and wayward immigrants, and generally elevating the economic, ethical, and moral consciousness of their members.

The best possible way to describe the various ideologies common to Finns in Michigan is to use a heuristic device. Because we live in a society that reads from left to right (and for no other reason), let us envision a left to right linear, colored spectrum, starting on the far left with the color black. Black Finns were a part of the radical union the Industrial Workers of the World (IWW). Black Finns espoused government dissolution in favor of a worker-controlled society. The Preamble to the Constitution of the IWW best explains the oft-misunderstood Wobbly ideology:

> The working class and the employing class have nothing in common. There can be no peace so long as hunger and want are found among millions of the working people and the few, who make up the employing class, have all the good things in life. Between these two classes a struggle must go on until the workers of the world organize as a class, take possession of the means of production, abolish the wage system, and live in harmony with the Earth.[123]

To some extent, all other organizational groups in Finnish America were at odds with the Wobblies because every other group had some type of organized governmental bureaucracy. Taking a small figurative step to the right, Red Finns espoused radical change through revolutionary means, but the maintenance of bureaucratic governance. Red Finns are often characterized as Communists with a big "C," but a large number of Finns believed in communism with a small "c." The difference is that big C communism was an actual system of government, while small c communism was an ideology or set of principles.[124]

Another ideological step to the right brings us to Yellow Finns. This group believed in dynamic change, but through parliamentary procedure. Yellow Finns were social democrats and liberals that differed substantially in their application of working toward economic and social change. Black and Red Finns often employed or at least espoused the use of direct action or physical force to change the social setting, while Yellow Finns sought change through the vote. Next are Pink Finns. Pink Finns were Christian socialists. They believed that Christ lived and taught principles of socialism through his ministry, but parted ways with other socialists on Marx's historic materialism.[125]

Finally, we have White Finns, the oft referred to Church Finn. White Finns sought maintenance of the current social milieu. The Lutheran Church had been the center of Finnish life in Finland, and White Finns believed this system worked well. White Finns also believed in working within the capitalist system as opposed to exploding it, which brought them into direct conflict with radical elements of the Black and Red Finns in Michigan. As a direct result of their working within the system, Black, Red, Yellow, and Pink Finns often accused White Finns of support for the company (big business) perspective.[126] We must also not forget another group that often gets little attention, the folks who did not join any groups. Many Finns understandably did not want anything to do with all the divisions and fractioning and avoided affiliation with any group, including the church. Additionally, many Apostolic or Laestadian Lutherans' religious beliefs did not condone associations with any of the various organizations.

In this chapter, we will attempt to give a broad historical analysis of the organizations representing the Finns in Michigan. Additionally, we will explore the divisions of the divisions, looking at fractioning of like-minded ideological groups. We must recognize that these groups were by no means fixed. People likely vacillated between groups within the span of a lifetime. Perhaps a person joined a group hoping to court affection from a certain someone and then left when the amorous connection failed to materialize. On the other hand, perhaps a person began to doubt the dogma of a certain group and left to explore different viewpoints. Neither these groups nor the people they represented were static, but rather very dynamic in membership and institutional relations. We will begin the analysis of this fractioning with the first group to fraction, religious organizations.

Religious Groups

Lutheranism was by far the most prominent denomination among Finnish immigrants. Devotion to the tenets of Martin Luther and the Reformation was the guiding religious philosophy in Finland. This Lutheran theosophy followed the Finns to America, but once in the New World the somewhat unified Lutheranism of Finland split into four main factions. In chronological order of divergence, they were the Apostolic Lutheran Church (often generally referred to as Laestadians), the Suomi Synod, the Finnish National Evangelical Lutheran Church in America, and independent Finnish Lutheran churches in America.

The first Finns to settle in the Copper Country did so on Quincy Hill, named after the Quincy Mining Company. The first small congregation of Finns in Michigan occurred in this industrial setting at a place of worship that consisted of Swedish, Norwegian, and Finnish parishioners. The Scandinavian Evangelical Lutheran Church, known to its members as the *"Norske, Quaener og Svenske Kireken"* (Norwegian, Kven—an ethnic Finnish group in northern Norway and Swedish Church) organized as a multi-ethnic congregation. Norwegian pastors administered to the multi-ethnic flock and interpreters relayed the sermons in Finnish to the "Quaeners" within the congregation. While this multi-ethnic set-up worked for some time, a split in the overall ethnic harmony was in the offing. A foreshadowing of this split was perhaps seen in how the various parishioners referred to the church. The Finns and Swedes referred to the church as the Scandinavian Lutheran Church, but the Norwegians referred to it as the Norwegian congregation.[127]

Not only was the small congregation of Scandinavians on Quincy Hill multi-ethnic, it was also multi-denominational within the realm of Lutheranism, at least within the congregation's Finnish population. Included in the Quincy Hill flock were Finnish Lutherans who identified with the national Lutheran Church in Finland as well as Laestadians, who identified with the Lutheran revival movement of Lars Levi Laestadius. A naturalist from Pajala in northern Sweden, Laestadius founded this branch of Lutheranism as a sort of back-to-the-land, nonmaterialistic movement. Laestadianism included strict abstinence from trappings of the material world, including dancing, gambling, and alcohol. Alcohol was an especially reviled transgression and the title of Laestadius's pastoral thesis, completed in 1843, signifies his disgust with alcohol: *Crapula Mundi* or *The World's Hangover*.[128] Among other facets of Laestadian practice are customary sermons by laypersons, communal or public confession of sins, and worship in unblemished, austere churches.[129]

The Laestadian contingency of the congregation soon became distressed with the doctrinal teachings and alleged materialism of Norwegian minister Pastor Roernaes. For his part, Roernaes had little patience for the pious religious scrutiny of the church's Laestadian members.

In 1872, unable to get along with the Laestadians, Roernaes upped the stakes and refused to give them some of the basic sacramental rights. This act pushed the Laestadians away from other Lutherans, including their fellow countrypersons who remained in the Scandinavian Lutheran church for a time, leading to a rift that exists to the present day. Once on their own, the Laestadians formed their own congregation that also began cleaving, reconciling, and again splitting.[130] From these early splits, many more splits occurred intradenominationally, and they continue to occur as of 2004, with the splitting of the Grace Apostles.[131]

Laestadians are often seen as conservative on many social issues, but it is significant that many Laestadians were involved as strikers in the 1913–14 Copper Country strike. Sadly, this disclosure comes from the fact that many of the Finns that died in the Italian Hall disaster in Calumet were likely Apostolic Lutherans. An examination of the names of those who died in the hall reveals that many of the surnames originated in the northern parts of Finland. Adding to this familial connection, services for many of the dead Finns from Italian Hall came at the Old Apostolic Lutheran Church on Pine Street in Calumet.[132]

Michigan has been especially influential in the development of the Apostolic and Laestadian Lutheran churches in America. Due to their intense fractioning, in the early to mid-1970s there were at least five Apostolic or Laestadian branches functioning in Michigan and along with the labor-political movement, Apostolic and Laestadian churches split more often than any other Finn organization in Michigan. While they fractioned frequently, their importance to maintaining Finnish ethnic heritage in Michigan cannot be understated. In many instances, Apostolic and Laestadian congregations have been torchbearers for Finnish culture and language, in large part because of their piety and reverence for Laestadius's ecclesiastical legacy in northern Finland.[133]

The next Lutheran body to split from the Scandinavian church in America was the *Suomi Synodi*, or Finland Synod. This group was the archetypical White Finn. The Suomi Synod attempted to maintain direct ties with the national Lutheran Church in Finland. For a long time it was the largest Finn organization in Michigan, but the Suomi Synod's early development did not occur in the state. In 1886, the Synod's first meeting toward organization was held in Minneapolis, Minnesota, when J. K. Nikander, J. J. Hoikka, William Williamson, and Karl Bergstadius met with J. Eisteinsen of the Norwegian Hague Synod to plan a governing body for Finnish Lutherans in America. Another interesting figure, J. W. Eloheimo, came from Finland later and added a curious dimension to the fledgling Synodian movement in America.

The efforts to bring about a board to serve the religious polity sputtered until December 17, 1889, when Eloheimo, Nikander, and Kaarlo Tolonen, a pastor from Ishpeming, met in Hancock to form a consistory or sort of executive committee.[134]

In March of 1890 the Suomi Synod became an official organization and Hancock became the headquarters of the Synod. Among the lay leaders of the early church body was the future second vice president of the malfeasant Finnish American Mining Company, J. H. Jasberg. From the start the Synod and its delegates were, in the words of Finnish American historian and Pastor Douglas Ollila Jr., a "traditionalist, conservative element in the immigrant population, and were inclined to favor a paternalistic church and clergy."[135]

The Synod's first constitution was very authoritarian. A clause ferreted out by reviewer Ino Ekman stated that the church could seize property of the individual congregations by force, if necessary. The early days were beset with administrative problems, but Nikander acted as the moderate to Hoikka and Eloheimo, guiding the Synod through tough times. Perhaps the most bizarre turn of events was when Eloheimo, then pastor of the Ironwood flock, declared himself the sovereign to usher in the second coming of Jesus Christ. Without doubt, the proclamation turned some heads. As Ollila, Jr. wrote:

> Strange stirrings were fomenting in his [Eloheimo's] mind and before long he engaged in paroxysms of mystical rapture in the form of special revelation. Before long, a bizarre document appeared written in English and titled "Proclamation of the Universal Kingdom during the Chiliad to Come." Its apocalyptic character was not so unusual; it was rather the fact that both the angel Michael and Jesus Christ revealed to humble minister William Elohim that he had been chosen by God to usher in the universal kingdom before the second coming of Christ. . . . Elohim was not only given sovereign power in life and death in the theocracy, but he was also to build a kingdom of peace and love where there were no taxes and where men worked an eight-hour day.[136]

It did not take the judicious folks at Synod headquarters long to put two and two together and presuppose that William Elohim was Eloheimo. His declaration, the Synod noticed, elevated Eloheimo to places where mortal men were not to go. Not long after Eloheimo anointed himself the sovereign of the second coming, he "resigned" from his position as leader of Ironwood's church. However, the parishioners in Ironwood called for his return, and why not, as many were laborers who likely saw Eloheimo's vision of no taxes and an eight-hour day as a slice of heaven on Earth.[137]

The Synod consistory rejected this plea, even after Eloheimo made an emotional speech at the 1892 church convention, in which he implored the Synod to publicly confess their transgressions against *him*. The Synod rejected his readmission to the ministerium. The ensuing rancor over the Ironwood congregation's meltdown forced the Synod to rethink its constitution. The Synod's new constitution was friendlier toward individual congregations, but much of the power remained in the hands of consistory . . . and a new clause added that, "the provisions for an unchangeable constitution were omitted in the *new* constitution."[138]

At the turn of the century, despite the Synod's problems, it had amassed 6,210 members, and that number rose to 15,413 (tallies include men, women, and children) by 1918, though Ollila, Jr. noted that these numbers are likely inflated. The Synod also added a theological college designed to train pastors for Finnish-language service in the United States and later added a commercial department to the college's theological curriculum. Suomi College, founded 1896 in Hancock, was a symbol of growth and prosperity and, coupled with the Finnish Lutheran Book Concern, a printing and publishing outfit begun in 1896, the Suomi Synod became a formidable purveyor of soul saving in America to many, but not all, Finns in Michigan.[139]

Critics of the Suomi Synod and its clergy argued that the church overlooked the economic and cultural conditions of many of its potential parishioners. This alleged ecclesiastical indifference to the plight of the working class and the socioculturally inclined (with the exception of a few Synod pastors such as William Rautanen) opened the door for other religious and secular organizations to administer to the cultural, economic, and spiritual needs of Michigan's Finns. As Ollila, Jr. wrote:

> One of the Synod's limitations was her rigid definition of herself as an authentic offshoot of the Church of Finland. Once she imposed that image upon herself, she found it impossible to be very tolerant of viewpoints other than her own. Industrial workers were naturally alienated and fellowship with others became impossible. She was very often suspicious of the fine

cultural efforts of the Kaleva lodges and Nikander even argued that clergy-
men should not involve themselves in temperance societies.[140]

Despite the Synod's problems relating to specific sections of the Finns in
Michigan, it did grow greatly within the Finn religious community, especially
in Michigan. By 1920, the Suomi Synod claimed fifty-six congregations from
Allouez-Ahmeek in the far north to Detroit in the far south and from Ironwood in the far west to Sault Sainte Marie in the east.[141] A credit to the growth
and sustainability of the now-defunct Suomi Synod is Finlandia University.
Despite recurring financial problems from its early history as Suomi College, Finlandia University provides the only private liberal arts education
in Michigan's Upper Peninsula and maintains a strong connection with the
Evangelical Lutheran Church both in America and in Finland.

Eloheimo, the previously introduced "religious sovereign," was a busy
man and is the reason for the next and last partition of the affiliated Finnish
Lutheran Churches in America. In 1890, before his visions, Eloheimo was
the pastor of a Suomi Synod church in Calumet. When a number of parishioners in the Calumet church opposed joining the fledgling Suomi Synod,
Eloheimo excommunicated five hundred members of the congregation.
Shortly after this, the Synod transferred Eloheimo to the Ironwood congregation, but the five hundred excommunicated members of the Calumet
church formed the roots of the "Peoples' Church," or *Kansalliskirkko*. The
Peoples' Church was a direct response to the hegemony and power vested
by the Suomi Synod in its consistory and pastors and thus away from individual people and congregations. The Peoples' Church was a congregation-
ally controlled church. It was very much a populist, democratic American
institution, though it never amassed the number of people the Suomi Synod
registered in Michigan.[142]

During its early years, the Peoples' Church was a loose affiliation of
independent churches, but in an amazing set of coincidences, Eloheimo
became the president of the Peoples' Church in 1898, when the independent
congregations officially bonded together as the Finnish National Evangelical Lutheran Church in America (FNELCA). Unlike the Suomi Synod, the
Peoples' Church did not seek an affiliation with the national Lutheran
church in Finland and early on supported affiliation with organized labor.
The irony in Eloheimo's presidency is that the FNELCA was likely home to

around five hundred people whom he had excommunicated from the Synod in 1890. Eloheimo, almost predictably, grew disinterested in the Peoples' Church because of doctrinal differences and left to administer independent congregations in Wyoming around 1900. He died "out west" in 1913.[143]

Much like the Suomi Synod, which merged with the Lutheran Church of America (which later merged to become the Evangelical Lutheran Church of America—ELCA) in the early to mid-1960s, the Peoples' Church moved to merge with an American body, but did so much earlier than the Suomi Synod. Due to a lack of trained Finnish-language pastors and shrinking ethnic language congregants (in 1948 membership in Michigan was 2,205 and in 1960 1,386), the Peoples' Church approached the Missouri Synod of Evangelical Lutheran churches in 1923. The president of the Missouri Synod attended the meetings at which the merger came into discussion, but no association was in the offing due to a single sticking point, women's right to speak and vote in church affairs. The Peoples' Church allowed the practice, but the Missouri Synod did not, and the merger fell though. A later merger didoccur, but not until 1964.[144]

Of course, wrapped in all the splitting were independent Finnish Lutheran churches that affiliated with none of the three main church bodies. Additionally, a few of the Finns in Michigan joined non-Lutheran, but Protestant denominations such as the American Congregational Church, the Methodist Church, and the Baptist Church.[145]

Finn Halls

As churches were incredibly important tangible structures to their congregations and the development of religion in the Finnish community in Michigan, Finn cultural and social halls were the most vital physical aspect of secular organizations. The halls served as meeting places, as venues for athletic competitions, and as theaters for plays and debates. The first Finn organizations in Michigan to build halls were the temperance societies. These halls quickly became the focal point and social nexus for activity within Finnish communities in Michigan. According to Finnish American historian Carl Ross:

> They [halls] were meeting places for congregations without churches, for clubs without buildings, and held officially banned, but tacitly sanctioned

Group photograph of the Köntys gymnastics society, Ironwood, Michigan, ca. 1920.
Courtesy of Finlandia University's Finnish American Historical Archive, Historic Photograph Collection.

dances. They were home to mutual aide societies where accident and burial insurance funds were collected. People flocked to temperance halls and became involved in a fantastic network of activity. There were speakers' clubs for training and practicing public speech, they read, recited and developed their talent for entertainments and festivals. Performers wrote and spoke poetry. There were drama groups in larger urban centers. Temperance halls were the location of lending libraries where local writers entered in annual essay contests."[146]

In Michigan's mining regions, halls were centers of refuge in an industrial tempest for many involved in the labor movement and quickly became a social core in Finnish immigrant enclaves both urban and rural:

> At the club [local socialist hall] they read their literature, discussed their
> problems, heard lectures, put on plays, sang, danced, flirted, romanced
> were married, celebrated the birth of children, had parties, became ill,

died and began the procession to cemeteries. At the halls, the miner was able, for a while, to forget his backbreaking toil and his problems of loneliness in what seemed to be a hostile world. He met with his own people, reminisced about the homeland, spoke of his aspirations and vented his hostility against a system which he thought prematurely robbed him of his manhood. As more women began to bring a semblance of civilization into the community, the Hall acted as a center for their lives as well. The one room shack, which many of them called home was drab and uninviting; it was a respite for them to get to the Hall to meet with other women, to put a dent into their homesickness and loneliness.[147]

Halls were epicenters of activity and thus became hotly contested possessions by splitting secular factions. Warring factions in the labor/political movement went all the way to court to take control of the Negaunee Labor Temple in 1913. The Red Finns won out in the end, gaining an injunction against the Finn Wobblies of the Negaunee Socialist local.[148] Halls were an indelible part of the Finn experience in Michigan and their importance, as tangible elements of the various groups they housed, cannot be overstated.

As halls were an important part of the organizational experience for Finns in Michigan, a certain type of Finn developed who cared less about the didactic ideology of the hall's group and more about having a good time. The Finns who reveled in the social experiences at the hall became known as "Hall Finns." This drew the ire of hardcore organizational adherents, but with talented musicians and well-orchestrated plays and performances gracing a hall's little stage, it was hard to turn a blind eye or deaf ear to the hall's entertainments.

One of the most famous hall entertainers was Viola Turpeinen of Champion and later Iron River, Michigan. Born on November 15, 1909, in Champion, Viola began playing the two-row button box at a young age. She was somewhat of a virtuoso and began playing the more complex piano accordion in her early teens. Viola honed her abilities at local Iron River halls, playing both the Finnish Worker's Hall and the Italian Bruno Hall. At the tender age of sixteen Viola was discovered by another Upper Peninsula Finnish musician named John Rosendahl. He became a sort of bandmate, manager, and promoter as he and Viola toured throughout the western Great Lakes region.

Viola Turpeinen, ca. 1930. Courtesy of Finlandia University's Finnish American Historical Archive, The Reino V. and Vienna H. Laine Collection of William Syrjälä and Viola Turpeinen Materials from Jeffrey C. Laine.

They later moved to Harlem, New York, which had a large Finnish community at the time. There they began playing to the thousands of Finns on the East Coast in the winter and touring through areas of established Finn settlements in the Midwest over the summer months. In New York, the duo added a member, another young female Finn accordion virtuoso from Ironwood's Norrie Location by the name of Sylvia Polso. With Viola and Sylvia's great music skills and good looks, coupled with Rosendahl's affable personality, good looks, and quick wit, the trio became a celebrated act in Finn Halls as well as for multi-ethnic crowds across the United States. The trio became so popular they signed a record deal with nationally known Victor Recording Company.[149]

A recollection from an appearance in Sault Sainte Marie's Thompson St. Finn Hall indicated that the trio's show was a multimedia event:

> Following a musical number by Miss Turpeinen and Miss Polso on accordions, and Mr. Rosendahl on the violin, slides of Finland were shown. . . . Mr. Rosendahl, on the violin, played an old folk song, and gave a very humorous speech. Another solo by Miss Turpeinen which was very well received concluded the first part of the program. . . . After the intermission,

during which coffee was served by the ladies, dancing was enjoyed until midnight, the music being furnished by the three visitors.[150]

Viola and Rosendahl were known to be romantically linked, but his drinking wore on Viola and perhaps their other band mate as well. In 1933, after Rosendahl died from a fall down a flight of stairs in New York City, Sylvia left the band to play at posh restaurants and hotels, while Viola began a lifelong partnership, both musically and intimately, with William Syrjälä. Syrjälä was a practical, hardworking brass horn player and percussionist from Cloquet, Minnesota. Viola and Bill began touring working-class halls and venues across the Eastern and Midwestern states through the Depression era as the "Turpeinen Trio" along with an unknown piano player. In 1952, the two moved to Lake Worth, Florida, from New York City and settled into a permanent gig at the Finnish Worker's Educational Club, while intermittently touring through their old stomping grounds.[151]

On December 26, 1958, Viola succumbed to a battle with breast cancer. In Bill's 1959 Day Book in an entry under January 1, the practical Finn musician wrote, "No dance tonight. Viola had her funeral on Tuesday, Dec. 30th, casket $575."[152] Bill's outward no-nonsense mentality likely hid his highly sentimental penchant, as a color photograph in the Finnish American Historical Archive shows an aged Bill holding an unopened postal package of Viola's ashes outside his Lake Worth home in 1992. Bill died in 1996 and was not able to witness Viola Turpeinen Syrjälä's induction into the Michigan Music Hall of Fame, Polka Music Category, on September 16, 2001.

Temperance Groups

The temperance movement was extremely popular in Finn social culture in Michigan, but like almost every other Finn organizational group in Michigan, it split into factions. The Finn temperance movement in America initially began as part of the Scandinavian Good Templar movement in the early 1880s. As more Finns joined the movement, the call to begin a Finnish-language branch of the movement began. The first Finn temperance society in Michigan formed in Republic. The temperance folks in Republic translated the by-laws of the Scandinavian Good Templar movement into Finnish and distributed copies among other upstart Finn temperance societies. As

Finnish-language temperance groups organized in places such as Calumet, Hancock, Ishpeming, Marquette, Atlantic Mine, Ironwood, and Bessemer, the groups decided to form a central governing body. They named this body the Finnish National Temperance Brotherhood, or *Suomalainen Kansallis Raittius Veljeys* (SKRV).[153]

In some manner, the early SKRV was an extension of White Finn ideals. It was socially very conservative, and dancing, pool playing, and other entertainments likely found in a bar were not permitted. This conservative attitude came under direct scrutiny in 1889 when the Calumet branch of the SKRV brought a motion to change the by-laws of the group to lessen the "don'ts" associated with the organization. The liberal Calumet society was especially at odds with restrictions against dancing and the directive that each meeting should begin with a prayer. The controlling conservative elements of the SKRV did not budge and dismissed the Calumet society from the organization. The breakaway Calumet group had supporters, and their exodus brought about an awakening of sorts, leading to the formation of a new, liberal branch of the temperance movement called the Friends of Temperance.[154]

Outwardly, the divisive issues were dancing and pool playing, as Samuel Ilmonen, a prominent White Finn, wrote in 1911: "At first the youth wanted only to stage very innocent parlor games, like chairs in a ring, then came exchanging couple's games or square dancing and finally came ballroom dancing."[155] In actuality, the organizational rift was much deeper than differences over parlor games and dancing. A cleft between older, socially conservative elements and younger, progressive elements divided the temperance movement. Many of the temperance societies' younger members saw the environmental and social ills around them in materialistic terms. To many liberal temperance members' way of thinking, the unequal distribution of wealth led to social problems such as intemperance, greed, and poverty. To the liberal element, prayer and religious rhetoric did not seem to be elevating the moral compass of wayward members of the Finn working class. Across Michigan, the same liberal discontent began to take shape, as Ilmonen wrote of Hancock's temperance society:

> A group began to grow to appeal for a more free-wheeling type of activity;
> these advocates came from among newcomers. A cleavage grew up in the

membership and the division became evident in even the most prosaic affairs. The North Star's membership was divided, in one section the serious ideologists, rule-keeping conservatives and in the other, those who were not yet recognized to be free-thinkers, but nevertheless, appeared to be reactionaries and resisters.

The youth were enamored by thespian pursuits. We had resisted the addition of a stage and scenery when the hall was enlarged, but now temporary moveable scenery began to appear in the hall. This was a clear omen of a new dawn, as yet, lacking in clarity, but with advance hues of a red sunrise.[156]

By the early to mid-teens, socialists began to infiltrate and take over the temperance societies and thus the beloved temperance hall. In many instances, the socialist elements used sheer mass to wrestle ownership of the hall from their conservative, teetotaling brethren. Helen K. Leiviska recollected:

You see what happened with a lot of these temperance societies was the majority would be the so called socialists and then they would vote the whole temperance society into the Socialist Party . . . And, I don't think hat would create very good feelings.[157]

Thus, the temperance movement was a sort of early incubator for the workers and political movements that would redefine the visage of the Finns in Michigan. Through the temperance societies the socialist and labor organizers had a hall, a built-in body politic, and temperance publications to advertise the merits of the fledgling Finnish socialist movement. The conservative temperance movement would bounce back and in some instances thrive, but the temperance societies gave the early socialist and unionist Finns access to a public forum and material culture before they could muster either on their own.

One of the most influential women in Finnish American history, a devout teetotaler and conscientious business person had a run-in with the Finnish immigrant socialists, but instead of a hall, the socialists wrestled an entire island settlement away from her. Margareeta (Kreeta) Niranen, better known as Maggie Walz, came to the United States from the Tornio River area, Oulu,

Maggie Walz, ca. 1910, organizer of Drummond Island colony and influential Copper Country Finnish immigrant businessperson. Courtesy of Finlandia University's Finnish American Historical Archive, Historic Photograph Collection.

in 1881. Maggie was deeply devoted to a life steeped in Christian temperance ideals. She was a member of Hancock's *Pohjantähti* (North Star) Temperance Society, a member of the Michigan Women's Christian Temperance Union, and a United States delegate to the International Women's Christian Temperance Union. Her temperance work ostensibly led to activity in the women's suffrage movement, study at Valparaiso College in Indiana, and the founding of the Calumet (Michigan) Finnish Women's Society, a group aimed at elevating the intellectual and social pursuits of Finnish immigrant women.[158]

Maggie was truly a triple threat advocate for women's rights because in addition to her temperance and suffragette work, she added adept business acumen to the promotion of women's socioeconomic independence. Maggie began life in America as a domestic, but saved and built profitable business ventures in Michigan's Copper Country. Over the course of her life, she was a store clerk at a Jewish American–owned general store in Hancock, a newspaper publisher, a job placement coordinator, a business manager, a real estate developer, and a land agent. Her role as land agent led to perhaps the most colorful period of her life. Maggie began a project to colonize a tract of land on Drummond Island, which lies just off the shoreline of the eastern Upper Peninsula in Lake Huron. Her colony began with high ideals; a place to assert the benefits of cooperative capitalism, founded on temperance and Christian ideals, with plans to expand the island's operations from agricultural endeavors to the development of a sawmill, brickyard, and flourmill.[159]

She began the venture by becoming a land agent for the U.S.' government and then invited select people to populate Drummond Island from a list of volunteers. Maggie's island settlement, Kreeta (named after her), was doomed to fail, however. The sandy, loamy earth that made up much of the island's thin topsoil led to disaster on the agricultural front and soon many left the island, irritated with Maggie for promoting a bad deal. Those who stayed organized a socialist local, which took control of the island in 1914. After the socialists came to power, Maggie cut all ties with her utopian enterprise.[160]

Maggie was a steadfast crusader for women's rights and temperance, but she also showed the dichotomy of the progressive Finnish mind. At this time in history, advocating extension of the vote to women was an incredible shock to male-dominated America. It was nothing less than a radical transformation of the American social order, but socialism went too far. Maggie Walz was progressive, but to a point. She brazenly drew away from her own creation when the "Reds" came in, illustrating the great complexity of the Finnish immigrant reaction to perceived problems in American society.

Labor and Political Groups

Labor and political groups split like every other group and to some extent at a much more rapid pace than other Finn organizations in Michigan. The working-class labor and political movements developed in the Finn communities of Michigan because many Finns recognized the vast disparity between the haves and the have-nots. These Finns became conscious of the fact that the people who produced the wealth, the workers, did not get the same compensation as those that controlled the wealth, the bosses. The response from Finn working-class organizations was to combat economic and social inequities with material explanations of class structure and collective organization. This is where working-class organizations differed greatly from church groups. Finn labor and proletarian political groups worked to change the social system in place on earth, not wanting to wait for rewards bestowed in the hereafter.

Organizations that represented the working class hardly began as highly ideological institutions. In fact, the first labor organizations among Michigan's Finns could best be described as workingmen's fraternal societies, hardly the radical, Marxist organizations some would become. In the early days of the working-class movement in Michigan, it was entirely possible to be a member of a church, a temperance society, and a workingmen's group. The first such workingmen's association, aligned with the liberal Imatra Societies of Finns on the East Coast, formed in Hancock, Michigan, as the *Jousi Seura,* or Society of the Bow, in 1900.

In 1904, the liberalism of Michigan Finns' early working-class organizations like the *Jousi* took a radical left turn with the introduction of the *Työmies* newspaper and its firebrand editor, Vihtori Kosonen. Kosonen and other *Työmies* staff members advocated a strict interpretation of Marxism, supported alignment with American working-class movements such as the Socialist Party of America, the Industrial Workers of the World and the Western Federation of Miners, and took a critical stance against religion in proletarian movements.[161]

In 1906, many local Finn socialist groups from across America came together in Hibbing, Minnesota, to form the Finnish Socialist Federation. This amalgam of local Finn socialist societies included as part of their membership a mixture of Black, Red, Yellow, and Pink Finns. Two years earlier, in 1904, the Finnish socialists joined the Socialist Party of America and in doing so, became the first and largest foreign-language party in American socialist ranks. Over time, though, the radicalism of the movement increased. Debate and rancor ensued between the groups, with the radical elements gaining control of the movement and its newspapers. As the radical elements came to power, they began to squabble and a split began to develop between the Red Finn socialists and Black Finn Wobblies.[162] This split between competing radical factions was already noticeable by the 1909 Finnish Socialist Federation meeting in Hancock, Michigan. Two figures especially stood out among the sparring factions. Frank Aaltonen of Negaunee symbolized the Red element, while the Work People's College's Leo Laukki, an enigmatic firebrand, bore the torch for the Finn Wobblies.

Finns in the labor movement likely flocked to proletarian organizations because many were not citizens of the United States and thus could not vote or participate in the elections of people who sought to control the conditions of their labor. The IWW especially espoused direct action that likely appealed to these immigrant workers because as Wobblies they were able to have an impact upon their own working conditions, wages, and industrial relations that was not linked to voting, which they could not do anyway. Direct action was the most important tool used by the IWW, and members of the IWW have recognized the Finn workers' contributions to industrial unionism.[163]

The organizational efforts of Finn IWW members were lauded in a Grammy-nominated album by Utah Phillips and Ani DiFranco titled *Fellow Workers*. In the song "Direct Action," Phillips recounted the Finn contribution to wind milling or street speaking, a practice in which Wobblie organizers would get on a soapbox in the middle of a street or sidewalk to make a speech. To paraphrase the song, Wobblies were often arrested by the police, who (they contend) were in the pockets of the companies the Wobblies were protesting. Though deficient in language, according to Phillips, Finns caught on to the precept of direct action quickly: "The Finnish worker learned enough English to say, 'Fellow Workers,' and if the cop wasn't there to arrest them, they'd say, 'Where's that damn cop.'"[164]

While greater goals held the Finn radicals together for a time, the stress of the 1913–14 Michigan copper strike tore the tense union between Red and Black Finns apart. After the 1913–14 Michigan Copper strike, many of the Finn Wobblies in Michigan relocated to Duluth, home of the Work People's College. Minnesota became the hotbed of Finn radicalism in the Midwest leading to the IWW led 1916 Minnesota Iron Miners' strike, but a significant number of Red Finns remained in Michigan, especially in Upper Peninsula agricultural communities on the industrial periphery. During this time, many Yellow Finns joined mainstream political parties after becoming disillusioned with the course of socialism. After the Red Finn-Black Finn split, the Finn Wobblies remained on a collective course, but still more splits came within the Red Finn movement.

There were several crises within the Red Finn movement, but perhaps the most destructive came when Joseph Stalin ordered the disbanding of the Workers Party of America's (later known as the Communist Party-United States of America) foreign-language federations. The largest of these foreign-language federations was the Finnish Federation of the Worker's Party. Many Finns would not sacrifice their ethnicity and Finn Hall culture for Stalin's goals. A mass defection of Finns from the Worker's Party of America occurred

Detroit Workers Club Brass Band, ca. 1921. Työmies Society 40 Vuotta.

in 1924. This terminal split in the Finn Communist parties of Michigan affected Communist locals from North Hurley to Sugar Island to Detroit. The splits forever divided communistic Red Finns from the Workers Party of America ranks, and lost to the Communists in America were many Red Finn halls, Workers Party brass bands, rank-and-file memberships, and Young Communist League youth organizations.[165]

Those Finns that left the Communist Party in many cases continued to espouse the ideology, but as small "c" communists, leaving the party behind, never to return to international communism. Those that stayed in the party remained stalwart supporters of Josef Stalin. Arvo Halberg was one such Finnish American who remained faithful to the ideals of the Communist Party in America. Many Americans better knew Halberg as Gus Hall, the son of Finnish immigrants from northeastern Minnesota. Gus Hall moved to the forefront of the party, becoming a leader in the party over time as its general secretary.[166]

Two unique occurrences with vastly different ideological backdrops greatly affected the Finn working-class movements in Michigan. They were terrorist activities by a branch of the Ku Klux Klan in small Finn agricultural communities in the Upper Peninsula and immigration of communistic Finns to Soviet Karelia in an appalling episode known as "Karelian Fever."

The Ku Klux Klan, organized as "Local Americanization Committees," invaded Finn agricultural locales around the Bruce Crossing area in the mid-1920s. The KKK used its usual scare tactics and intimidation ploys such as cross-burning and racist epithets to scare local residents believed to be involved in "leftist" movements. There was, however, no reported physical violence resulting from KKK activities. Purportedly, the life of the KKK in these areas was short-lived, but their presence in areas of Michigan's Upper Peninsula indicated that the Finn working-class movement was significant enough to warrant attention from groups like the KKK that wished to destroy ethnic heritage and the working-class movement.[167]

Karelian Fever, the other heartbreaking incident, was a literal movement of North American Finns to Soviet Karelia, which was historically an ethnic Finn and Karelian settlement within annexed boundaries of the Soviet Union. Hundreds of working-class Finns left Michigan to build a proletarian paradise in the vast forests of Soviet Karelia, only to be executed in the purges of the maniacal Soviet dictator Josef Stalin. The Soviet bureaucracy separated families and imposed a reign of terror on Finns from Michigan and North America who simply wanted to develop a working-class state in Karelia. Soviet police, the NKVD, picked thousands of ethnic Finn men, women, and children from their beds in the middle of the night and sent them to gulags or shot them.

An oral history conducted by Dr. Alexey Golubev of Petrozavodsk, Russia, with Dagne Salo, a Finn from Covington, Michigan, whose family moved to Karelia during the Great Depression, recounts the distress of living in a state of constant fear: "During 1937 and 1938 we almost never slept at nights." Dagne recalled that her father was judged to be an enemy of the people and ". . . a spy. My God, I don't know how such a person could be. . . . After that I was branded as the daughter of an enemy of people. I always responded: 'Tell me, enemy of what people? He is from these people!'" When asked how people were targeted by the Soviet police, Dagne stated, "Evil tongues. There were many of such loyal Stalinists, you know. . . . They looked at me in such a manner, and forbade [their children] to communicate with me, and never communicated with me themselves—for them, it was shameful, for I was the daughter of an enemy of people."[168]

Through the ups and downs, ebbs and tides of the various working-class movements of the Finns in Michigan, a base survived. This base endured even when the movement had to disappear from sight for extended periods during Red Scares of the 1920s and later through McCarthyism. Sigrid Lepisto, wife of the Suomi Synod's Rev. Antti Lepisto, indicated in an oral history, "I know that when Antti was at Mass, Michigan, there was a school teacher there . . . he said they (Red Finns) all went underground."[169] Through suppression at the federal, state, and local levels, and to the detriment of their constitutional rights, the socialist and communist movements of the Finns in Michigan carried on in the struggle to redefine society in an image they believed represented a more just society.

Finnish American elements of working-class organizations exist to this day, but as shells of their former selves. The Työmies Society exists, but with perhaps a different sense of radical purpose from the days of its founding, and Finnish North American members of the IWW still organize workers. A unique feature of the Finn working-class movements was that from very early on, they tried to join American movements while maintaining a sense of ethnic identity within English-language organizations.[170] As the seemingly inevitable process of assimilation set in, radical, progressive, and liberal elements of the Finn working class in Michigan joined American working-class institutions. They joined organizations like the Communist Party-USA, the Socialist-Labor Party, the Congress of Industrial Organizations (CIO), the Farmer-Labor Party, the American Federation of Labor (AFL), and the Democratic Party, choosing to fundamentally engage in broader American working-class issues and political parties as *Americans* of Finn heritage.

Cooperative Groups

The importance of the cooperative movement in Finnish America cannot be understated and thus the prominence of Finn Coops in Michigan was widespread. Arnold Alanen, Finnish American landscape historian, wrote about the coop movement in the Finnish population of the Upper Great Lakes: "Whereas the Finns are popularly known for introducing the sauna to America . . . It could be argued that one of the most legible stamps of Finnish American influence has been in the development of consumer's cooperatives."[171]

Advertisement for Red Star Cooperators' Best Coffee, sold under this label throughout coop stores in Michigan until after the 1929 split in the Finn cooperative movement. Cooperative Pyramid Builder, 1927.

In their earliest stages, cooperatives organized to help miners or other industrial workers survive through the lean times of strikes, and as such, the cooperative movement became closely associated with the workers' struggle to obfuscate the capitalist system.[172] As miners were blacklisted and moved to agricultural areas, the proletarian consumers' coops they depended on during strike times followed into the countryside. The rural coop became an important fixture in Finn farming communities. To the many Finns who came to depend on the coop, it became a way of life. Families and individuals shopped, worked, ate, and were entertained at the local coop; it was an integral part of the Finn experience in Michigan.

The cooperative movement in Finnish America borrowed from the basic tenets of England's Rochdale Cooperative principles. The five most significant guiding principles were: "1–each member of the cooperative has one vote no matter how many shares they own in the coop. 2–the profits made by the coop will be returned to members in proportion to their consumption of coop goods and services. 3–No person should be excluded from membership because of color, religion or political beliefs. 4–A fixed percentage of profit will be used to educate the public about cooperatives. 5–The continuous expansion principle states that coop will expand when able to provide goods and services members need and when possible secure access to raw materials." [173] Interestingly, though supposedly steeped in social equality, for a time Finn Coop stores offered consumers goods in four grades or hierarchies, Red Star ("Cooperators best"), Blue Star, White Star, and Yellow Star. This grading of goods seemed hardly in line with the egalitarian principles of the movement.

In the mid to late 1920s, the coop movement started to diversify in both goods and services as well as in membership. Recognizing the need to draw in other ethnicities, the coops' powerful publishing branch began to print magazines and newspapers in the English language. In addition, new and innovative associations joined the traditional consumer's store. The New Era Life Association of Grand Rapids, Michigan, a life-insurance company, advertised in the *Co-operative Pyramid Builder,* illustrating the Finn Coop movement's desire to spread and support expansion of the cooperative mission in Michigan.[174]

By the mid-1920s, Finn consumers' coops in America and Michigan became incredibly successful proletarian business ventures and thus attracted the attention of Communist bureaucrats in Moscow who hoped to tap into the success of the Finn coop movement. The Comintern, the international branch of Soviet organization, created an occasion for a bitter schism in the movement when they called for the return of a small percentage of coop profits in America to the Soviet Union. This bitter divide, which occurred in 1929, splintered the Finn coop movement into Red and White factions.[175]

The pre-split coop movement had centralized its activity in Superior, Wisconsin, under the name Central Cooperative Exchange in 1918, and after the split occurred the White coops retained the Superior premises and became the Central Cooperative Wholesale (CCW). The Red coops relocated their wholesale to another location in Superior, becoming the Farmers' and Workers' Cooperative Unity Alliance. Therefore, many communities in Michigan, even small rural communities had two coop stores, the Red coop and the White coop.[176]

The Red Finn cooperators continued to link the movement directly with the revolutionary working-class struggle, while the White coops functioned as apolitical cooperatives. As Martin Kaurala, one-time employee of the Mass City Coop, wrote, "The Unity Alliance and its affiliates held to the basic principle that the cooperative movement should be part and parcel of the class struggle movement, not a purely business enterprise as the CCW. This internal split was unfortunate and weakened the movement."[177]

Tension was often palpable and residents of divided towns based their social lives on which cooperative was home base, but like many things in daily life, quality of goods on hand often superseded ideology. As Frank Walli remembers from his experience managing the Red coop in Bruce Crossing: "a lot of the Settlers' Cooperative [White coop] people used to come over to our Co-op just to buy the flour. Because they wanted the Unity Alliance flour because it was unbleached and a very good flour."[178]

By the Depression era and into the 1940s, the all-inclusive White coops, still linked to some extent with elements of the working-class movement, grew in membership rapidly. The Red coops did not fare as well, with the possible exceptions of the Eben Junction and Mass City area's coops, which thrived for some time, lasting through the repressive McCarthy era and into the early to mid-1960s. In 1955, the Central Cooperative Wholesale's White coops tallied 20,167 members in thirty-one societies in Michigan, surpassing the membership of all other Finn organizational groups in Michigan.[179]

The largest of Michigan's White coop ventures were not traditional consumer's cooperative stores, but rather service associations such as the Alger Delta Co-op Electrical Association, with 2,318 members, and the Stephenson Marketing Association, with 2,246 members. The largest consumer's cooperatives were in Hancock, with 2,185; Rudyard, with 1,183; Bruce Crossing, with 1,127; Trenary, with 1,114; and Sault Sainte Marie, with 1,073 members.[180] It should be noted though that by this time non-Finns or people with partial Finn ethnicity had joined the immigrant Finn cooperative ranks, swelling the membership of the Finns' White coops.

The White coop movement had taken its place as the largest organizational group of the Finns in Michigan, but this dominance was fading. As the immigrant and first-generation Finns passed away, as supermarkets came on the scene in Michigan, and as the Upper Peninsula's agricultural areas began to wither, the long-standing importance of the coop declined as well. Today, a handful of cooperatives stand as testaments to the Finn coop era. A few former White Finn coops remain in small agricultural areas, like the Settler's Coop in Bruce Crossing, the Trenary Coop in Trenary, and the Chatham-Eben Coop in Chatham. Folks can still become members in these working-class ventures that were one of the most significant Finn organizations in Michigan.

The Knights and Ladies of Kaleva

Often associated with middle-class businesspersons, the Knights and Ladies of Kaleva were founded as a group to celebrate Finnish heritage and elevate the conditions of Finns in America. Their lodges, known as *majas* for the men and *tupas* for the women, were named after characters and places from the Finnish national epic *The Kalevala*. The men's group came into existence in 1898, with their first lodge established in Belt, Montana. The women's group came along a bit later in 1904, established in Red Lodge, Montana. Michigan became home to several lodges of the Knights and Ladies, but because membership in the Knights and Ladies was by invitation only and somewhat exclusive, the membership rolls of the *majas* and *tupas* never included large numbers. Hancock and Calumet were the first to organize lodges in Michigan, beginning in 1899, and other lodges soon followed in commercial centers across the Upper Peninsula in towns like South Range, Ironwood, Negaunee, and Ishpeming, to name a few. As the membership grew, lodges began to spring up in rural areas as well.[181]

The Knights and Ladies are a bit of an outlier within the history of the Finns in Michigan because the Knights and Ladies were the only Finn organization not to split, but they came close several times. The founder of the Knights was John Stone, born in Oulu, Finland, in 1865 and buried in South Range, Michigan. Stone, considered a man of vision, decided to found an order based on knowledge and accomplishment, virtues he thought would elevate the consciousness of the Knights' members. He was also apparently very irritable and liked to cuss, as a Knights' history stated: "John Stone . . . was a hot-tempered and fiery man who may have used improper expressions in his speech, but so did many other people." The Knights eventually dismissed their own founder from the order in 1928 and this brought the Knights close to splitting, but cooler heads prevailed and the order readmitted him, healing relations.[182]

Stone founded the Knights with two unique caveats: that the foundation of knowledge and accomplishment would occur with Finnish culture and that it would occur in a secretive fashion, with a full slate of rites and rituals. Therefore, as it were, the Knights became a sort of Finnish Freemasons.[183] As the organization added lodges, the need to form a central governing body became apparent. The men and ladies created Upper Lodges known as *Ylimajas* and *Ylitupas*, respectively, and elected high officials known as

Finnish Immigrant Press

The Finnish-language press in Michigan was a staple in the immigrant community. All the various Finn factions and partitioned organizations in Michigan published their own newspapers and periodicals. Between 1876 and 1913, Finn publishers in America printed more than eighty newspapers. The first Finnish-language newspaper in America, printed in Hancock, Michigan, in 1876, was *Amerikan Suomalainen Lehti-American Finnish Newspaper.** From this early paper, many others followed. The Suomi Synod printed the *Amerikan Suometar* in Hancock. The Peoples' Church printed *Auttaja* in Ironwood. The Apostolic churches printed *Valwoja* and *Opas* in Calumet. Temperance organizations printed yearly periodicals and the Knights and Ladies of Kaleva printed the *Kalevainen,* a periodical.

Arguably, the most influential of the Michigan Finns' newspapers was *Työmies,* a labor newspaper published in Hancock. Perhaps the most impressive fact about *Työmies* is that it began in Hancock (after moving from Worcester, Massachusetts) as a small publishing venture with fewer than one thousand subscribers in 1904, but grew to a massive mouthpiece for the Socialist Party of America by 1912 with twelve thousand subscribers, almost thirty staff members, a large bookstore, three outlet distributors in Ishpeming, Duluth, Minnesota, and Virginia, Minnesota, and two publishing buildings spanning three addresses on Franklin Street in downtown Hancock. The paper continued to grow and reached maturity on the eve of the 1913–14 Michigan copper strike, but then had its subscriber based cleaved almost in half after the strike over dissension between Red Finns and Finn Wobblies. As a result of the split, *Työmies* relocated to Superior, Wisconsin, in 1914, and the Finn Wobbly faction began publishing their own newspaper, eventually to become known as *Industrialisti,* in Duluth, Minnesota.†

* Työmies Society, "Early Finnish American Newspapers in U.S.A.," in *Työmies: Seventieth Anniversary Souvenir Journal, 1903–1973* (Superior, Wisc.: Työmies Society, 1973), 18.
† Kaunonen, "Conflict in the Copper Country," 76–121.

the *Ylin Pappi*, or High Priest, for the men and the *Ylin Emäntä*, or Supreme Matron, for the women.[184]

The Knights and Ladies' secret society was met with suspicion by some members within communities in which they lived and worked.[185] As we have already discussed, non-Finns in many communities saw Finns as clannish and isolated, having strange sociocultural practices; add to this mysterious doings of a secret society and the Knights and Ladies probably seemed like an anomalous bunch. The Knights and Ladies also fell into conflict with the Evangelical Lutheran church movement because pastors, especially Suomi Synod and Apostolic Lutheran pastors, saw the rituals of the Knights and Ladies as being rooted in anti-religious paganism. This dissension subsided for the most part by the 1960s.[186] The Knights and Ladies of Kaleva exist to this day, though their numbers have decreased substantially in Michigan. The group's activity has shifted from secretive meetings and rituals to a torchbearer's role in promoting Finnish and Finnish American ethnic identity through publicized activities and the granting of scholarships to college bound students. Possibly because of this newly defined role, the exclusive nature of the group has almost disappeared and membership is open to Finnish Americans from across the economic and social spectrums.

Conclusion

While the Finns' contributions to Michigan are vast and varied, perhaps the most important contribution of the Finns in Michigan was to future generations of Finnish Americans in the state. The immigrant and first-generation Finns toiled in the mines, mills, factories, farms, and fields so that following generations could have the opportunity to ascend the American socioeconomic ladder.

Again, it is important to remember that not all of the Finns in Michigan were hardworking, sober toilers struggling to make life better for their kids and their kids' kids, but for the most part the early Finns in Michigan cut a path that led to a better life for the next generations. An excellent example is in education; many children and grandchildren of Finnish immigrants went into this field. Note the faculty and staff at Michigan's institutions of higher learning, especially Upper Peninsula universities such as Northern Michigan University, Michigan Technological University, and of course Finlandia University, or administrators and teachers at the secondary and elementary level; you will notice many Finnish Americans. The men who worked in the mines, the women who labored in the homes of the wealthy, and the subsistence farm families that struggled to make a living on meager repasts and brow sweat gave the generations to come the chance at a better life.

One person who received the benefits of his parents' toil was Emil Hurja, known as the Wizard of Washington. Hurja, born in 1892 in Crystal Falls, Michigan, is reportedly the only person from the Upper Peninsula to ever appear on the cover of *Time* magazine. Hurja was the private pollster of Franklin D. Roosevelt and provided the statistical acumen that drove Roosevelt's victorious campaigns. Hurja was a large part of Roosevelt's Democratic machine, but when Roosevelt tried to pack the Supreme Court with justices of his choosing, Hurja dissented and turned Republican to directly challenge Roosevelt's administration. Hurja lost his first election, but added to Republican strategists' ability to operate effective polling operations and thus helped that party win back congress during the mid-1940s. Hurja had an incredible impact on the nation's history.[187]

As Finnish immigrants became more familiar with America, their children became quick-study Americans. Assimilation into the "American lifestyle" often occurred at rapid rates and once the extractive industries, logging camps, and small farming communities began to lose their economic viability, many Finns from the Upper Peninsula began the migration to urbanized areas of downstate Michigan, which contained smaller (proportionally) populations of Finns. The southeastern Lower Peninsula and especially the greater Detroit area received, at various times, influxes of second-, third-, and fourth-generation Finnish Americans. This downstate migration accelerated the assimilation process as Finns came into more frequent contact with "others."

Assimilation had many facets, social, cultural, religious, and of course familial. Perhaps more than any other circumstance or institution, marriage assimilated many Michigan Finns into American society. As Finns migrated from entirely Finnish settlements in the Upper Peninsula to southeastern Michigan, they invariably encountered a large number of non-Finns and inevitably "discovered" members of the opposite sex from other cultures, ethnicities, and religious denominations. To be sure, this integration with other peoples happened in the Upper Peninsula as well, and the Detroit area had its Finnish enclaves within the region that preserved facets of Finnish ethnicity in the urban southeast, but Detroit could perhaps best be described as an urban fusion that erased many a cultural and ethnic boundary; for as many know, the lure of love does not know Finn from Norwegian or even Irish-Catholic, as a 1972 oral history interview with James O'Meara documented:

Of course when I first met Lydia in Detroit at the Graystone Ballroom, when I first asked what her name was she said it was Saukko; well in Detroit, with a great number of Polish people there, I was boarding in a house adjacent to the Polish section, it seemed anybody with a lot of Ss and Ks and Zs was Polish. So, I thought she was Polish. Of course it didn't make a difference whether she was Eskimo, Polish or what, but it was hard to believe and that was the first time I had met a Finn.[188]

James married Lydia in 1928, and this type of union often created a rather common new religious dynamic, "Finn-Catholics."

Sports were also an important part of the assimilation of many Detroit area Finnish Americans. Detroit's *Voima* (Strength) athletic club was a key part of making the Labor Sports Union, a working-class association that promoted the merits of competition through amateur athletic events, a nationally significant organization that federated in 1927. *Voima* was uniquely positioned to propel the Labor Sports Union into a nationwide organization because *Voima* had exemplary access to facilities and was somewhat centrally located in the center of Finnish America. At this time, *Voima* owned a large gymnasium, had access to an auditorium owned by Detroit's Finnish Educational Association that seated some seven hundred people, and also had access to the facilities of Loon Lake Cooperative Park for games, matches, and festivals. Loon Lake often took center stage as host for the Labor Sports Union's events; it hosted track meets, calisthenics drills, gymnastics expositions, swimming competitions, field events, and even a summer school dedicated to teaching athletics and coaching athletes.[189]

By 1927, assimilation had permeated the Finnish experience in the Detroit area (and Michigan) so much that many of the games and contests attractive to the Labor Sports Union members were American team games like baseball, softball, and basketball. Additionally, as the popularity of the Labor Sports Union grew, other ethnicities joined Finnish Americans on the courts and fields of athletic competition. In 1928, looking to broaden participation, the Labor Sports Union and Detroit's Finn community hosted an indoor track meet that welcomed Hungarians, Ukrainians, Swedes, Czechs, and Americans into athletic competition with the sons, daughters, and grandchildren of Finnish immigrants.[190]

By the 1940s, Finnish Americans had not only assimilated into American society, but they had also, to some extent, climbed several rungs on America's socioeconomic ladder. They began to enter the American middle class. This ascension to the middle class was perhaps most conspicuous in the southeastern part of the state, where better wages and benefits through union membership, employment in white-collar professions, and organization of socioeconomic prospects around a prosperous auto industry catapulted many Finnish Americans and their families into the middle class. In his article "The Finns in Michigan," Pastor John Wargelin of the Suomi Synod writes in a 1940 issue of *Michigan History Magazine:*

> [In Detroit] they are employed at various trades, some of them having distinguished themselves as draftsmen and engineers and originators of important improvements, while their children occupy clerical or commercial positions. Several young men, and even young women, serve on the Detroit police force. There are several professional men among them, e.g., doctors, dentists, lawyers, teachers, artists and ministers [also business owners].[191]

Seemingly, Wargelin's predisposition toward the Suomi Synod prevented his mentioning of the contributions of Finn labor, political, and cooperative organizations in Detroit. These organizations, the first Finnish immigrant institutions in Detroit, paved the way for many future generations of Finnish American working-class families to garner the comfort of "modern" homes, find an identity within the American labor movement during watershed events like the 1937 Flint Sit-down Strike, send their children to college, and afforded many the ability to purchase the very cars they helped build on assembly lines. Both the Finnish American labor-political movements and the corresponding coop movement had solid, but developing foundations in 1930s Detroit, as a 1929 *Pyramid Builder* article conferred:

> Detroit co-operators have opened a new store at 13701 Woodrow Wilson, corner of Grand.
>
> Maurice Raeburn, well-known Co-op. manager, is in charge of the store and gives his opinion that in Detroit and nearby cities there can be developed one of the largest and strongest co-operative movements in America.

Propaganda is vital in a large city like Detroit as only through publicity can people be made acquainted with the principles of co-operation. Even conscious co-operators living in the city do not know yet of the existence of the store and the great mass of workers must be informed of the co-operative and what it represents.

The days from Saturday, May 4th, to Sunday, May 12th (1929), have been set aside as "Detroit Co-operators' Week" and will begin with an entertainment and dance at the Finnish Labor Temple, 14th and McGraw Ave., in the evening of May 4th. The program will include the Finnish operetta "Sorrento" under the direction of John Ahti who has been popularly termed the "Workers' Tenor" throughout the Northwest. Other numbers will include presentations by the Workers' Chorus, solos, recitations, and speeches in both English and Finnish. During the week, demonstration days will be held at the store to introduce "Red Star" Soups and Coffees to the patrons, and a mass picnic at the Loon Lake Co-operative Land Association's grounds on Sunday, May 12th, will end the "Week."[192]

The assimilation and progression to the middle class did not come easily for some first- and second-generation Finns in Michigan. The "tween" generations often faced difficult challenges. These "tween" children of Finnish immigrants were literally between two worlds. At school, many got a slap on the knuckles with a ruler if a teacher heard Finnish in the classroom. At home, they had to speak Finnish because mom and dad or the grandparents could not understand English. Additionally, were they Finns or were they Americans? Perhaps there was also guilt caused by turning away from the culture of parents and grandparents in favor of Americanization.

While many in the first and second generations felt the pressure to assimilate, later generations of Finnish Americans also felt the converse, the longing to maintain some semblance of their ethnic heritage. Two recent phenomena are tangible displays of the maintenance of Finnish ethnicity in the state of Michigan. The first is a large summer festival called FinnFest. According to FinnFest USA's website, it is "committed to engaging members of our community with our rich culture and history through relevant programming and events."[193] FinnFest's programs and events, organized locally under the supervision of FinnFest's national nonprofit governing board, are nondenominational or unaffiliated with any one political or religious group.

While FinnFest is a festival that celebrates Finnish ethnicity, its organizers invite and openly welcome other nationalities to the celebration, mostly to help eat the copious amounts of delicious food prepared for the event.

Organized in 1982, FinnFest's first gathering was in Minneapolis, Minnesota. Since then, various sites within the United States that have significant Finnish American populations have hosted the event. Michigan, of course, has hosted its fair-share of these summer festivals. The first Michigan Finn-Fest was held in Hancock, which hosted the event in 1985. Livonia hosted it in 1987; in 1990, Hancock hosted again; 1996 found Marquette as the festival's host; and in 2005 Marquette hosted Finn *Grand* Fest, a joint festival of United States and Canadian Finns. The 2005 Marquette festival had many amenities, one of which was the world's largest sauna, in which hundreds of festival-goers took in the healing power of steam together.

The other phenomenon is an Upper Peninsula Finnish American institution known as *Suomi Kutsuu* or *Finland Calling*. Hosted by Carl Pelonpaa and produced by Marquette's WLUC TV-6, *Suomi Kutsuu* is a cherished link for Finnish Americans that maintains the bonds of second-, third-, and fourth-generation "Finnishness." Pelonpaa, born in 1930 to Finnish immigrants, worked for nine years in Ishpeming area iron mines, played some pro-level baseball, and then served in the U.S. Army for two years. Pelonpaa's big break in media came in 1959, when he hosted a radio show, and then in 1961 he became a weatherman for TV 6. *Suomi Kutsuu*'s beginnings, in 1962, were thanks to an advertising ploy by a Marquette-area travel agent. In order to sell trips to Finland, *Suomi Kutsuu*, it was thought, could do the promoting, calling many first-, second-, and third-generation Finnish Americans back to the Old Country.[194]

While the beckoning of Finland was cause for origination of the show, dances drove the success of the program. Pelonpaa organized and attended dances throughout the Upper Peninsula, the largest of which occurred in South Range (in Michigan's Copper Country) with over eight hundred people attending the event. These dances fueled the interest that would propel *Finland Calling* to become a staple of many Finnish American cultural lives. In addition to dances, Pelonpaa organized trips to Finland and Scandinavia, fulfilling the original mission of the broadcast's initiation, and physically linking Finnish Americans to Finland through travel. In 2000, Pelonpaa was inducted into the Michigan Music Hall of Fame in the polka

music category because, "Without a doubt, Carl Pelonpaa's 'Finland Calling' program is one of the longest running and most successful television
programs in Michigan."[195] Pelonpaa still conducts much of the program in
the Finnish language, with a required sprinkling of Finglish to guarantee the
show's authenticity as a truly Finnish American institution.

■ ■ ■

The Finns in Michigan have an interesting and complex history. In this
book, we have looked at some of the broad outlines and nebulous contours
of the "Finn" experience in Michigan. If you found the material in this
book interesting, please see the following bibliography for further reading.
Connecting to the past is essential for many reasons, but perhaps the most
important motive is that the future is never as bright as when the past has
been illuminated.

Also, please note the number of oral histories used in this book. Oral history is, in my opinion, an underused historical tool. The best thing about
"doing oral history" is that you do not have to have hours of training, read
hundreds of books, or even go to a university to be good at it. Read up and
interview your family members. I guarantee grandma did something interesting in her twenty-somethings, grandpa was more than the man who gave
you candy, and Uncle Toivo did not always just sit in the corner and cuss at
the dog. We *owe* these folks who came before us our attention, interest, and
time. Do not let history textbooks published by large corporate conglomera-
tions dictate to you what your history is . . . make it yourself. Sit down and
interview grandma or grandpa, burrow through the closet with them, and
above all else, ask questions—the elders will dig it.

As we have seen, many of the Finns in Michigan faced tough challenges,
and struggled to make it in their new homeland. The history of Finns in
Michigan is a vibrant, rich, and incredibly relevant history that demonstrates
not only the power an immigrant people can have in shaping a sense of community in a new environment, but also the influence an immigrant people
can have in affecting the greater society in which they live. The Finnish experience in the state was not passive. Finns influenced Michigan history as
much as Michigan affected the history of its Finns. It is a testament to their
work, cultural organizations, and lives that we still discuss their contributions (good, bad, and ugly) to the exciting history of Michigan's peoples.

Finnish American Cultural and Historical Societies in Michigan

- Finlandia University's Finnish American Historical Archive, 601 Quincy Street, Hancock, MI 49930; (906) 487-7347; *archives@finlandia.edu*

The Finnish American Historical Archive is the oldest and largest repository of Finnish North American materials in the world. The repository began collecting materials in 1932 and with the generosity of its donors has assembled a unique and vast collection of research materials. The repository's collections contain a broad spectrum of materials that represent the complexity of Finnish America. The archive's collections include materials about Finnish North Americans involved in the Industrial Workers of the World, the Communist Party, the Socialist Party, cooperative movements, the Knights and Ladies of Kaleva, Evangelical Lutheran churches in America, Laestadian movements, and many other groups.

Academic and scholarly researchers, family historians (genealogists), and the general public use the archival collection to connect, discover, learn, and research the eclectic history of Finnish America The Finnish American Historical Archive collects materials and publications relating to Finnish North American organizations, individual Finnish North Americans, Swede-Finnish North Americans, Kven North Americans and Sámi North Americans. The archive also collects historic materials from Finland in an attempt to maintain the contextual history of Finnish immigration. Because of its mission as a family history center, the archive also accepts genealogical materials from Finnish North America, Swede-Finnish North America, and Finland, Sweden, northern Norway, and Lapland.

- Finlandia University's Finnish American Heritage Center, 601 Quincy Street, Hancock, MI 49930; (906) 487-7302; *www.finlandia.edu/Department/FAHC/fahc.html*
- Finnish American Society of West Central Michigan, 1663 5th Street, Muskegon, MI 49441; (231) 726-2816
- Finnish Center Association, 35200 West Eight Mile Road, Farmington Hills, MI 48335; (248) 478-6939; *www.finnishcenter.org*
- Finnish Theme Committee-Finlandia Foundation Copper Country Chapter; (906) 482-0248; *www.pasty.com/heikki/ftcinfo.html*
- Hanka Homestead, P.O. Box 58, Pelkie, MI 49958; (906) 334-2601 (summer only); *www.hunts-upguide.com/keweenaw_bay_hanka_homestead.html*
- Kaleva Historical Society, 14551 Wuoksi Avenue, Kaleva, MI 49645; (231) 362-3519
- Little Finland, P.O. Box 352, Hurley, WI 54534; (715) 561-4360; *www.littlefinland.com/default.asp*
- Upper Peninsula Chapter of the League of Finnish American Societies, Marquette, MI 49855; *ronjhi1138@aol.com*

"Finn" Recipes

Leipä juustoa (Finnish Squeaky Cheese)

10 qts. of raw milk
½ tablet of rennet
3 tsp. salt

Dissolve rennet in a little water and add to the milk. Milk should be kept warm at all times. Let the milk and rennet set 20–45 minutes, stirring occasionally. Add 3 tsp. of salt. After the milk has set, scoop the whey off as much as possible. Drain the remainder of the whey in a colander; when there is a mass of curds, flip it into a broiling pan. Broil in oven with the door open for about 15 minutes or until brown; flip onto flat pan, broil other side. This cheese is delicious when hot, but also good cold and lasts a few weeks in the refrigerator.

Pannukakku (Finnish Oven Pancake)

1 qt. milk
4 eggs
½ cup sugar

1 tsp. salt

1 cup flour

Mix all the ingredients. Place in greased baking pan; the liquid should be about ⅛" thick. Bake at 375° or until brown, 20–40 minutes. Eat it warm with sugar or jam on top.

Nisu or *Pulla* (Finnish coffee bread)

2 cup milk, scalded and cooled

½ stick butter or margarine, melted in milk

1–2 yeast cakes

4 eggs, beaten

1 cup sugar

7 cardamom seeds, peeled and crushed (1–3 tsp)

7–9 cup flour

1 tsp. salt

Prepare dough as you would any other bread. Be sure not to hurry it—let dough rest for fifteen minutes after all of the ingredients have been mixed. Let the dough rise to twice its size, punch down and let rise again. Divide dough into 3 parts, then divide these into 9 parts and braid loaf with 3 of the pieces. Place on greased baking sheet, let rise again for 20 minutes. Spread with beaten egg and sprinkle with sugar. Bake at 400° for 45 minutes or until brown. Dough is good for rolls, buns, etc.

Notes

1. Suomi College, *Suomi College Academic Catalog 1986–89* (Hancock, Mich.: Suomi College, 1985), 9.

2. Finlandia University, *Finlandia University Course Catalog 2007* (Hancock, Mich.: Finlandia University, 2006), 2.

3. Douglas J. Ollila, Jr., "The Work People's College: Immigrant Education for Adjustment and Solidarity," in *For the Common Good: Finnish Immigrants and the Radical Response to Industrial America* (Superior, Wisc.: Tyomies Society, 1977), 87–95.

4. *Vallankumous 1915* and *Suomi Opisto Fennia 1915*. Information and statistics gleaned from photographs and text.

5. Finlandia University Communications Department, *The Bridge: 2005* (Hancock, Mich.: Finlandia University, 2005), 16.

6. Viljo Niitemaa, "The Finns in the Great Migratory Movement from Europe to America 1865–1914," in *Finland Salutes U.S.A.: Old Friends—Strong Ties* (Turku, Finland: Institute of Migration, 1976), 65–80.

7. Ibid., 67.

8. Armas Holmio, *The Finns in Michigan* (Detroit: Wayne State University Press, 2001), 55.

9. Reino Kero, "The Background of Finnish Emigration" in *The Finns in North America: A Social Symposium* (East Lansing: Michigan State University Press,

1969), 55–58.

10. Eloise Engle, *The Finns in America* (Minneapolis: Lerner Publications Company, 1977), 11–15.

11. Ibid.

12. Matti Klinge, *A Brief History of Finland* (Keuruu, Finland: Kutannusosakeyhtiö Otavan painolaitokset, 1981), 50–63.

13. Engle, *Finns in America*, 11–15; Klinge, *Brief History of Finland*, 87–91; and Gary Kaunonen, "Conflict in the Copper Country: Building Toward a Strike in a Finnish Immigrant Neighborhood, Hancock, Michigan 1904–1914" (master's thesis, Michigan Technological University, 2007), 11–13.

14. Minnesota was second with 60,610, New York third with 27,247, Massachusetts forth with 26,889, and Washington fifth with 22,048. Ralph Henry Smith, *A Sociological Survey of the Finnish Settlement of New York Mills, Minnesota and its Adjacent Territory, Revised,* comp. Darrel G. Nicholson (Minneapolis: Snellington Publishers, 2005), 22.

15. Ibid., 74–77.

16. Holmio, *Finns in Michigan,* 42–45.

17. Ibid., 43–45 and 76–78.

18. Larry Lankton, *Beyond the Boundaries: Life and Landscape at the Lake Superior Copper Mines, 1840–1875* (New York: Oxford University Press, 1997), 64–65.

19. Larry Lankton, *From Cradle to Grave: Life, Work, and Death at Lake Superior Copper Mines* (New York: Oxford University Press, 1991).

20. Viktor Ollikainen to Hilja Fraki, personal correspondence, January 24,1913, Hilja Fraki Collection, Manuscripts Box T-53, Finnish American Historical Archive, Finlandia University, Hancock, Michigan.

21. Sandra Sarkela, interview by Elma Ranta, November 6, 1974, oral history interview transcript, Finnish American Historical Archive, Finlandia University, Hancock, Michigan, 2052.

22. Dave Engel and Gerry Mantel, *Calumet: Copper Country Metropolis* (Rudolf, Wisc.: River City Memoirs, 2002), 75. *Calumet: Copper Country Metropolis* is a collection of interesting news items culled from the pages of the *Copper Country Evening News* between 1898 and 1913.

23. Ibid.

24. Ibid., 83, 87, and 100.

25. Elou Kiviranta, "The Memory of Finland," translated by Aino Utriainen, Kiviranta Poetry Collection, Finnish American Historical Archive, Finlandia University,

Hancock, Michigan, n.d.

26. Keijo Virtanen, "Problems of Research in Finnish Re-emigration," in *The Finnish Experience in the Western Great Lakes Region: New Perspectives* (Turku, Finland: Institute of Migration, 1975), 202.

27. Ibid., 204–6.

28. Elsie M. Collins, *From Keweenaw to Abbaye: Biographical Sketches of a Community as Told to Elsie M. Collins* (Ishpeming, Mich.: Globe Printing, Inc., 1975), 23–26.

29. The distinction of Finns as "violence-prone revolutionaries" likely emanated from events such as the 1905 general strike against the Czar in Finland and set the stage for a dynamic history in labor relations with Michigan industry and moreover for interactions within Finnish communities themselves. Peter Kivisto, "The Decline of the Finnish American Left," *International Migration Review* 17, no. 1: 68.

30. Arnold Alanen, "The Corporate Mining Environment," in *Finnish Diaspora II: United States*, ed. Michael Karni (Toronto: Multicultural History Society of Ontario, 1981), 43–45.

31. Lankton, *From Cradle to Grave*, 211–12.

32. Matti Kaups, "Finnish Place Names in Michigan," *Michigan History* 51, no. 4 (1967): 347; and Holmio, *Finns in Michigan*, 76–143.

33. Matti Kaups, "The Finns in the Copper and Iron Ore Mines of the Western Great Lakes Region, 1864–1905: Some Preliminary Observations," in *The Finnish Experience in the Western Great Lakes Region: New Perspectives* (Turku, Finland: Institute of Migration, 1975), 55–56.

34. Lankton, *From Cradle to Grave*, 212–14.

35. Ibid., 30–32, 69–71, 212–13, and 111–13.

36. Ibid., 95.

37. Lankton, *From Cradle to Grave*, 210–13; and Kaunonen, "Conflict in the Copper Country," 23–25.

38. For more information on striking Finns see Lankton, *From Cradle to Grave*, chapter 13; Arthur Puotinen, "Copper Country Finns and the Strike of 1913," in *The Finnish Experience in the Western Great Lakes Region: New Perspectives* (Turku, Finland: Institute of Migration, 1975);and Kaunonen, "Conflict in the Copper Country." Kaups, "Finnish Place Names in Michigan," is credited with the quotation, 343.

39. Lankton, *From Cradle to Grave*, Puotinen, "Copper Country Finns," Puotinen,

"Copper Country Finns and the Strike of 1913," and Kaunonen, "Conflict in the Copper Country."

40. Lankton, *From Cradle to Grave,* chapter 13; and Kaunonen, "Conflict in the Copper Country."

41. Lankton, *From Cradle to Grave,* chapter 13; and Kaunonen, "Conflict in the Copper Country."

42. Kaunonen, "Conflict in the Copper Country," 155–61. . For more information specifically on Italian Hall, see Larry Molloy, *Italian Hall: The Witnesses Speak* (Hubbell, Mich.: Great Lakes Geoscience, 2004) and Steve Lehto, *Death's Door: The Truth behind Michigan's Largest Mass Murder* Troy, Mich.: Momentum Books, 2006).

43. Lankton, *From Cradle to Grave,* chapter 13; and Kaunonen, "Conflict in the Copper Country."

44. Kaups, "The Finns in the Copper and Iron Ore Mines," 70.

45. Holmio, *Finns in Michigan,*134.

46. Ibid., 135.

47. Ibid., 133–36.

48. Ernie Ronn, *52 Steps Underground: An Autobiography of a Miner* (Marquette, Mich.: Center for Upper Peninsula Studies, Northern Michigan University, 2000), 2–4.

49. Kaups, "The Finns in the Copper and Iron Ore Mines," 70.

50. Mr. and Mrs. Leonard Lahti, interview by Arthur E. Puotinen, August 3, 1973, oral history interview transcript, Finnish American Historical Archive, Finlandia University, Hancock, Michigan, 2.

51. Lynn Miller, ed., *A Collection of Recollections: Crystal Falls, Michigan, 1880–1980.* (Dallas, Tex.: Taylor Publishing Company, 1980), 103.

52. Holmio, *Finns in Michigan,* 127–32.

53. Frank Walli, interview by Douglas J. Ollila, Jr., August 8, 1973, oral history interview transcript, Finnish American Historical Archive, Finlandia University, Hancock, Michigan, 3078–79.

54. Annie and Leon Anderson, interview by Randy Maki, n.d., oral history interview transcript, Finnish American Historical Archive, Finlandia University, Hancock, Michigan, 1612–19.

55. Ibid.

56. National Geological Survey of Finland; J. H. Jasberg Collection, Manuscripts Collection, Personal and Family Papers, T-1a, Finnish American Historical Archive,

Finlandia University, Hancock, Michigan; and *Daily Mining Gazette* article, Finnish American Mining Company Vertical File, Finnish American Historical Archive, Finlandia University, Hancock, Michigan.

57. Mrs. Ralph Abrahamson, August 1, 1973, oral history interview transcript, Finnish American Historical Archive, Finlandia University, Hancock, Michigan.

58. National Geological Survey of Finland.

59. J. H. Jasberg to John Daniell, September 10, 1912, Manuscripts Collection, Personal and Family Papers, J. H. Jasberg Collection, T-1a, Finnish American Historical Archive, Finlandia University, Hancock, Michigan.

60. C. J. Jackola to J. H. Jasberg, June 25, 1915, Manuscripts Collection, Personal and Family Papers, J. H. Jasberg Collection, T-1a, Finnish American Historical Archive, Finlandia University, Hancock, Michigan.

61. Superior National Bank to J. H. Jasberg, September 4, 1920, Manuscripts Collection, Personal and Family Papers, J. H. Jasberg Collection, T-1a,Finnish American Historical Archive, Finlandia University, Hancock, Michigan.

62. C. J. Jackola to J. H. Jasberg, November 12, 1921, Manuscripts Collection, Personal and Family Papers, J. H. Jasberg Collection, T-1a, Finnish American Historical Archive, Finlandia University, Hancock, Michigan.

63. Arthur Thurner, *Strangers and Sojourners: A History of Michigan's Keweenaw Peninsula* (Detroit, Mich.: Wayne State University Press, 1994), 125.

64. Holmio, *Finns in Michigan,* 94–95.

65. Ibid.

66. Matti Kaups, "Finnish Place Names in Michigan," 338–40; and Holmio, *Finns in Michigan,* 162–63.

67. Reuben Niemisto, interviewed by Allan Lavery, January 30, 1974, oral history interview transcript, Finnish American Historical Archive, Finlandia University, Hancock, Michigan, 1008–9.

68. Arthur R. Erickson, interview by Michael Loukinen, October 5, 1974, oral history interview transcript, Finnish American Historical Archive, Finlandia University, Hancock, Michigan, 2163–65.

69. Ibid., 2165.

70. Ibid., 2171.

71. Ibid., 2182.

72. Annie and Leon Anderson, interview, 1611.

73. Holmio, *Finns in Michigan,* 148–49.

74. Ibid., 150.

75. George Rahkonen, "The Michigan Timber Workers' Strike," *Työmies-Eteenpäin*, July 1998, 13.

76. Ibid.

77. Ibid., 22.

78. Ibid.

79. Ibid.

80. Ibid.

81. Ibid.

82. Holmio, *Finns in Michigan*, 168–69.

83. Keijo Virtanen, "The Influence of the Automobile Industry on the Ethnic Picture of Detroit, Michigan, 1900–1940," in *Publications of the Institute of History, General History, University of Turku, Finland, No. 9* (Vaasa, Finland: Vaasan Kirjapaino Oy, 1977), 71–75.

84. Virtanen, "Influence of the Automobile Industry," 77–81.

85. Holmio, *Finns in Michigan*,168.

86. Virtanen, "Influence of the Automobile Industry," 80; and Michael Loukinen, "Second Generation Finnish-American Migration from the Northwoods to Detroit, 1920–1950," in *Finnish Diaspora II: United States* (Toronto: Multicultural History Society of Ontario, 1981), 110.

87. Ibid., 168.

88. Finnish Center Association website, http://www.finnishcenter.org, accessed August 3, 2007.

89. Loukinen, "Second Generation Finnish-American Migration," 113.

90. Ibid.

91. Ibid., 117.

92. Ibid., 113–115.

93. Kaups, "Finnish Place Names in Michigan," 344.

94. Collins, *From Keweenaw to Abbaye,* 1–2.

95. Ibid., 5–7.

96. Holmio, *Finns in Michigan,* 168–70.

97. Ann Marin, *Vernacular Architecture of Finnish Immigrants in the Central Upper Peninsula of Michigan,* unpublished paper, December 1980, Finnish American Historical Archive, Finlandia University, Hancock, Michigan, 5.

98. Marsha Elizabeth Penti, *Religious Identities in the Composition Class: Students of Difference* (PhD diss., rhetoric and technical communication, Michigan Technological University, 1998), chapter 4, 2–3.

99. Marin, *Vernacular Architecture,* 8.

100. Ibid., 9.

101. Ibid.

102. Ibid., 18–19.

103. Ibid.,19.

104. Ibid., 8.

105. Esther Savela Storhak and Lynne Golden Palo, *J.A. Doelle School Album* (self-published, n.d.), 15.

106. Ibid.

107. Thurner, *Strangers and Sojourners,* 145.

108. Sarkela, interview, 2060.

109. Ibid., 2058–59.

110. Beatrice Meyers, interview by Gary Kaunonen and Hannu Heinilä, July 27, 2006, Chassell, Michigan, oral history interview, nontranscribed interviews, Oral History Collection, Box 26, Finnish American Historical Archive, Finlandia University, Hancock, Michigan.

111. Ensio Bjorklund to Ruth Juntilla, Oskar, Michigan, June 28, 1923, Libby Koski-Bjorklund Collection, Individual Donor Collection, Historic Photograph Collection, Finnish American Historical Collection, Finlandia University, Hancock, Michigan.

112. Evelyn Turunen, interview by Elaine Loukinen, September 28, 1974, oral history interview transcript, Finnish American Historical Archive, Finlandia University, Hancock, Michigan, 2379–80.

113. Ibid., 2380–81.

114. Vienna Laine and Jeffrey Laine, interview by Gary Kaunonen, Escanaba, Michigan, March 23, 2007, oral history interview, tape 1, side 2, Oral History Collection, Box 26, Finnish American Historical Archive, Finlandia University, Hancock, Michigan.

115. Ibid.

116. Ibid.

117. Meyers, interview.

118. Ibid.

119. Ibid.

120. Gus O. Linja, *Copper Country Connections* (Kearney, Neb.: Morris Publishing, n.d.), 38–39.

121. Sheldon Jackson, General Agent of Education in Alaska, United States Depart-

ment of the Interior, *Eleventh Annual Report on the Introduction of Domestic Reindeer into Alaska* (Washington, D.C.: Government Printing Office, 1901), 1481–97; and Linja, *Copper Country Connections,* 39–42.

122. Linja, *Copper Country Connections,* 41–43.

123. Industrial Workers of the World, *Solidarity: Labor History Calendar of the Industrial Workers of the World, Centenary Edition* (Philadelphia: Industrial Workers of the World Publishing, 2005), back cover.

124. Color descriptions come from an aggregate of sources. For further in-depth reading on the complexity of the colors of Finnish immigrants, read Michael G. Karni, ed., *For the Common Good: Finnish Immigrants and the Radical Response to Industrial America;* Kivisto, "Decline of the Finnish-American Left"; Auvo Kostianen *The Forging of Finnish-American Communism, 1917–1924: A Study in Ethnic Radicalism* (Turku, Finland: Institute of Migration, 1978);, Arthur Puotinen *Finnish Radicals and Religion in Midwestern Mining Towns, 1865–1914;* and Gary Kaunonen, "Arvo Halberg/Gus Hall: The Making of an American Communist," unpublished senior thesis, Minnesota State University–Mankato, Mankato, Minnesota, 2003, Finnish American Historical Archive, Finlandia University, Hancock, Michigan.

125. Michael G. Karni, ed., *For the Common Good,* Kivisto, "Decline of the Finnish-American Left," Kostianen *The Forging of Finnish-American Communism,* Puotinen *Finnish Radicals and Religion,* and Kaunonen, "Arvo Halberg/Gus Hall."

126. Ibid.

127. Scandinavian Evangelical Lutheran Church Records, Finnish American Churches Box B-3, Manuscripts Collection, Finnish American Historical Archive, Finlandia University, Hancock, Michigan; and Holmio, *Finns in Michigan,* 173–75.

128. Aila Foltz and Miriam Yliniemi, eds., *A Godly Heritage: Historical View of Laestadian Revival and Development of the Apostolic Lutheran Church in America* (Frazee, Minn.: self-published, 2005), 20–21.

129. Ibid.; and Uuras Saarnivaara, *The History of the Laestadian or Apostolic-Lutheran Movement in America* (Ironwood, Mich.: National Publishing Company, 1947).

130. Ibid.

131. Foltz and Yliniemi, *Godly Heritage,*195–208.

132. Molloy, *Italian Hall,* 144–45; Engel and Mantel, *Calumet,* 211 (photograph of the inside of the church); Pirjo Mikkonen and Sirkka Paikkala, *Sukunime* (Helsinki, Finland: Otava, 19920; and Lankton, *From Cradle to Grave,* 238.

133. Foltz and Yliniemi, *Godly Heritage*, 195–208 and Holmio, *Finns in Michigan*, 181–83.

134. Douglas J. Ollila Jr., "The Suomi Synod: 1890–1920," in *The Faith of the Finns: Historical Perspectives on the Finnish Lutheran Church in America* (East Lansing: Michigan State University Press, 1972), 158–60.

135. Ibid.

136. Ibid., 162

137. Ibid.

138. Ibid., 162–63.

139. Holmio, *Finns in Michigan*, 202–4 and 395; and Ollila, Jr., "Suomi Synod: 1890–1920," 165–69.

140. Ollila, Jr., "Suomi Synod: 1890–1920," 168.

141. Holmio, *Finns in Michigan*, 202–5.

142. Ollila, Jr., "Suomi Synod: 1890–1920," 161–64;, and Douglas Ollila, Jr., "The Suomi Synod in Perspective" in *The Finns in North America: A Social Symposium* (East Lansing: Michigan State University Press, 1969), 191–94.

143. Ollila, Jr., "Suomi Synod in Perspective," 192–93; and Holmio, *Finns in Michigan*, 208–9.

144. Holmio, *Finns in Michigan*, 212–14.

145. Ibid., 215–18.

146. Carl Ross, "Essays on the Finnish American Community: 1865–1914, Part 2—The Finnish American Community Matures—1885–1900," Carl Ross papers, Immigration History Research Center, University of Minnesota, 5–6.

147. Arthur Puotinen, "Transitions for Finnish-American Workers in Temple and Marketplace," unpublished paper, December 7, 1970, Immigration History Research Center, University of Minnesota, 12.

148. Auvo Kostiainen, *The Forging of Finnish-American Communism, 1917–1924: A Study in Ethnic Radicalism* (Turku, Finland: Institute of Migration, 1978), 40.

149. James P. Leary, "The Legacy of Viola Turpeninen," in *Finnish Americana, Vol. 8* (New York Mills, Minn.: Parta Printers, Inc., 1990), 7–8.

150. Ibid., 8–9.

151. Ibid.

152. Ibid., 9; and William Syrjälä, Diaries, *The Reino V. and Vienna H. Laine Collection of William Syrjälä and Viola Turpeinen Materials from Jeffrey C. Laine*, Manuscripts Collection, Box Z-1a, Finnish American Historical Archive: Finlandia University.

153. Salomon Ilmonen, "North Star Temperance Society, Hancock, Michigan: 25 Year History, 1885-1910," in *Raittius-Kalenteri,* trans. E. Olaf Rankinen (1911; repr., Ishpeming, Mich.: Suomalainen Kansallis Raittius Veljeys, 1994), 1-3; and Holmio, *Finns in Michigan,* 237-39.

154. Holmio, *Finns in Michigan,* 239-43.

155. Ilmonen, "North Star Temperance Society," 5.

156. Ibid., 12.

157. Helen K. Leiviska, interview by Douglas J. Ollila, Jr., 1974, oral history interview transcript, Finnish American Historical Archive, Finlandia University, Hancock, Michigan, 9.

158. K. Marianne Wargelin Brown, "Maggie Walz: Entrepreneur and Temperance Crusader," in *Women Who Dared: The History of Finnish American Women,* ed. Carl Ross and K. Marianne Wargelin Brown, 151-57 (St. Paul, Minn.: Immigration History Research Center, 1986).

159. Ibid.

160. Ibid.

161. Arthur Puotinen, "Early Labor Organizations in the Copper Country," in *For the Common Good: Finnish Immigrants and the Radical Response to Industrial America,* 119-22 (Superior, Wisc.: Tyomies Society, 1977); Michael Karni, "The Founding of the Finnish Socialist Federation and the Minnesota Strike of 1907," in *For the Common Good: Finnish Immigrants and the Radical Response to Industrial America,* 65-70 (Superior, Wisc.: Tyomies Society, 1977); and Työmies Society, "Finnish Socialist Federation," in *Työmies: Seventieth Anniversary Souvenir Journal, 1903-1973,* 29-31 (Superior, Wisc.: Työmies Society, 1973).

162. Puotinen, "Early Labor Organizations in the Copper Country," and Karni, "The Founding of the Finnish Socialist Federation."

163. Ibid.

164. Bruce "Utah" Phillips and Ani DiFranco, "Direct Action" on *Fellow Workers,* Buffalo, N.Y.: Righteous Babe Records, 1999.

165. Gary Kaunonen, "Arvo Halberg/Gus Hall."

166. Ibid.

167. Settlers Cooperative, Inc. *75 Years, 1917-1992,* Settlers Cooperative, Inc.: Bruce Crossing, Michigan, 1992, 6-7 and Holmio, 353.

168. Dagne Salo, oral history interview, recorded and transcribed by Alexey Golubev, Petrozavodsk, Russia, September 21, 2006, National Archive of the Republic of Karelia, Petrozavodsk, Russia.

169. Mrs. Sigrid Lepisto, interview by Adrian A. Niemi, December, 4, 1974, oral history interview transcript, Finnish American Historical Archive, Finlandia University, Hancock, Michigan, 5.

170. Kaunonen, "Conflict in the Copper Country," 176.

171. Arnold Alanen, "The Development and Distribution of Finnish Consumers' Cooperatives in Michigan, Minnesota and Wisconsin, 1903-1973," in *The Finnish Experience in the Western Great Lakes Region: New Perspectives* (Turku, Finland: Institute of Migration, 1975), 104.

172. Ibid., 103-6.

173. Reino Nikolai Hannula, *Blueberry God: The Education of a Finnish-American* (San Luis Obispo, Calif.: Quality Hill Books, 1979), 212-14.

174. Central Cooperative Exchange, *Co-operative Pyramid Builder* 3, no. 2, February 1928.

175. Alanen, "Development and Distribution," 113-20; and Michael Karni, "Struggle on the Cooperative Front: The Separation of Central Cooperative Wholesale from Communism, 1929-30," in *The Finnish Experience in the Western Great Lakes Region: New Perspectives* (Turku, Finland: Institute of Migration, 1975), 186-201.

176. Alanen, "Development and Distribution," 113-20 and Karni, "Struggle on the Cooperative Front," 186-201.

177. Martin Kaurala, "The Mass Co-operative Company," *Työmies-Eteenpäin*, July 8, 1993, 21.

178. Walli, interview, 3088.

179. Central Cooperative Exchange, *Cooperative Pyramid Builder;* and Holmio, *Finns in Michigan*, 202-4.

180. Central Cooperative Wholesale, *1955 Coop Yearbook* (Superior, Wisc.: Central Cooperative Wholesale, 1955), 44-49.

181. Alfons Ukkonen, *A History of the Kaleva Knighthood and the Knights of Kaleva*, trans. Tessa Suurkukka (Beaverton, Ontario: Aspasia Books, 2002), 12-16; and Holmio, *Finns in Michigan*, 304-8.

182. Ukkonen, *History of the Kaleva Knighthood*, 13-15.

183. Holmio, *Finns in Michigan*, 304-5.

184. Kent Randell, "Knights of Kaleva Collection Finding Aide," Andrew Brask Correspondence, Box 20, Manuscripts Collection, Finnish American Historical Archive, Finlandia University, Hancock, Michigan; and Holmio, *Finns in Michigan*, 306.

185. Ukkonen, *History of the Kaleva Knighthood,* 15.

186. Ibid., 14–15; and Holmio, *Finns in Michigan,* 325.

187. Melvin Holli, *The Wizard of Washington* (New York: Palgrave Macmillan, 2002); and Emil Hurja, Vertical File, Finnish American Historical Archive, Finlandia University, Hancock, Michigan.

188. James O'Meara, interview by Arthur Puotinen, July 13, 1972, oral history interview transcript, Finnish American Historical Archive, Finlandia University, Hancock, Michigan.

189. Charles Jay, "The Labor Sports Union from a Detroit Perspective," in *Työmies-Eteenpäin 85, 1903–1988* (Superior, Wisc.: Työmies Society, 1988), 22–26.

190. Ibid.

191. John Wargelin, "The Finns in Michigan," *Michigan History Magazine* 24 (Spring 1940): 187.

192. Central Cooperative Exchange, "Detroit Co-operators Plan Big Program," *Cooperative Pyramid Builder* 4, no. 4 (1929): 122. In the October 1929 issue of *The Pyramid Builder* it stated that the Detroit Finnish Coop moved into the Labor Temple building at 5969 14th Street, near McGraw.

193. FinnFest USA, "Our Mission," www.finnfestusa.org/Our%20Mission.html, accessed April 11, 2008.

194. State of Michigan, "Michigan Music Hall of Fame-Polka Music Category; Carl Pelonpaa Hall of Fame Membership Certification," September 24, 2006.

195. Ibid.

For Further Reference

Abrahamson, Mrs. Ralph. Oral history interview transcript, August 1, 1973. Finnish American Historical Archive, Finlandia University, Hancock, Michigan.

Alanen, Arnold. "The Corporate Mining Environment." In *Finnish Diaspora II: United States*, edited by Michael Karni. Toronto: Multicultural History Society of Ontario, 1981.

———. "The Development and Distribution of Finnish Consumers' Cooperatives in Michigan, Minnesota and Wisconsin, 1903-1973." In *The Finnish Experience in the Western Great Lakes Region: New Perspectives*. Turku, Finland: Institute of Migration, 1975.

Anderson, Annie and Leon. Interview by Randy Maki, n.d. Oral history interview transcript. Finnish American Historical Archive, Finlandia University, Hancock, Michigan.

Björklund, Ensio, to Ruth Juntilla, Oskar, Michigan, June 28, 1923. Libby Koski-Björklund Collection, Individual Donor Collection, Historic Photograph Collection, Finnish American Historical Collection, Finlandia University, Hancock, Michigan.

Central Cooperative Exchange.*Co-operative Pyramid Builder* 3, no. 2, February 1928.

———. "Detroit Co-operators Plan Big Program," *Co-operative Pyramid Builder* 4, no. 4, 1929.

Central Cooperative Wholesale. *1955 Coop Yearbook.* Superior, Wisc.: Central Cooperative Wholesale, 1955.

Collins, Elsie M. *From Keweenaw to Abbaye: Biographical Sketches of a Community as Told to Elsie M. Collins.* Ishpeming, Mich.: Globe Printing Inc., 1975.

Engel, Dave, and Gerry Mantel. *Calumet: Copper Country Metropolis.* Rudolf, Wisc.: River City Memoirs, 2002.

Engle, Eloise. *The Finns in America.* Minneapolis: Lerner Publications Company, 1977.

Erickson, Arthur R. Interview by Michael Loukinen, October 5, 1974. Oral history interview transcript. Finnish American Historical Archive, Finlandia University, Hancock, Michigan, 2163–65.

Finlandia University. *Finlandia University Course Catalog 2007.* Hancock, Mich.: Finlandia University, 2006.

Finlandia University Communications Department. *The Bridge: 2005.* Hancock, Mich.: Finlandia University, 2005.

FinnFest USA. "Our Mission." www.finnfestusa.org/Our%20Mission.html (accessed April 11, 2008).

Foltz, Aila, and Miriam Yliniemi, eds. *A Godly Heritage: Historical View of Laestadian Revival and Development of the Apostolic Lutheran Church in America.* Frazee, Minn.: self-published, 2005.

Hannula, Reino Nikolai. *Blueberry God: The Education of a Finnish-American.* San Luis Obispo, Calif.: Quality Hill Books, 1979.

Holli, Melvin. *The Wizard of Washington.* New York: Palgrave Macmillan, 2002.

Holmio, Armas. *The Finns in Michigan.* Detroit: Wayne State University Press, 2001.

Houghton County Historical Society. *Big Louie Moilanen: Giant of the Copper Country.* Lake Linden, Mich.: John H. Forster Press, 1995.

Hurja, Emil. "Vertical File." Finnish American Historical Archive, Finlandia University, Hancock, Michigan.

Ilmonen, Salomon. "North Star Temperance Society, Hancock, Michigan: 25 Year History, 1885–1910." In *Raittius-Kalenteri,* translated by E. Olaf Rankinen. 1911. Reprint, Ishpeming, Mich.: Suomalainen Kansallis Raittius Veljeys, 1994.

Industrial Workers of the World. *Solidarity: Labor History Calendar of the Industrial Workers of the World, Centenary Edition.* Philadelphia: Industrial Workers of the World Publishing, 2005.

Jackson, Sheldon. General Agent of Education in Alaska, United States Department of the Interior. *Eleventh Annual Report on the Introduction of Domestic Reindeer into Alaska.* Washington, D.C.: Government Printing Office, 1901.

Jasberg, J. H. Manuscripts Collection, Personal and Family Papers, T-1a, Finnish American Historical Archive, Finlandia University, Hancock, Michigan.

Jay, Charles. "The Labor Sports Union from a Detroit Perspective." In *Työmies-Eteenpäin 85, 1903–1988.* Superior, Wisc.: Työmies Society, 1988.

Karni, Michael. "The Founding of the Finnish Socialist Federation and the Minnesota Strike of 1907." In *For the Common Good: Finnish Immigrants and the Radical Response to Industrial America.* Superior, Wisc.: Tyomies Society, 1977.

———. "Struggle on the Cooperative Front: The Separation of Central Cooperative Wholesale from Communism, 1929–30." In *The Finnish Experience in the Western Great Lakes Region: New Perspectives.* Turku, Finland: Institute of Migration, 1975.

Kaunonen, Gary. "Arvo Halberg/Gus Hall: The Making of a Finnish American Communist." Unpublished senior thesis, Minnesota State University–Mankato, Mankato, Minnesota, 2003.

———. "Conflict in the Copper Country: Building Toward a Strike in a Finnish Immigrant Neighborhood, Hancock, Michigan 1904–1914." Master's thesis, Michigan Technological University, Houghton, Michigan, 2007.

Kaups, Matti. "Finnish Place Names in Michigan." *Michigan History,* no. 4 (winter 1967): 51.

———. "The Finns in the Copper and Iron Ore Mines of the Western Great Lakes Region, 1864–1905: Some Preliminary Observations." In *The Finnish Experience in the Western Great Lakes Region: New Perspectives.* Turku, Finland: Institute of Migration, 1975.

Kaurala, Martin. "The Mass Co-operative Company." *Työmies-Eteenpäin,* July 8, 1993.

Kero, Reino. "The Background of Finnish Emigration." In *The Finns in North America: A Social Symposium.* East Lansing: Michigan State University Press, 1969.

Kiviranta, Elou. "The Memory of Finland." Translated by Aino Utriainen. Kiviranta Poetry Collection, Finnish American Historical Archive, Finlandia University, Hancock, Michigan.

Kivisto, Peter. "The Decline of the Finnish American Left." *International Migration Review* 17(1983): 1.

Klinge, Matti. *A Brief History of Finland.* Keuruu, Finland: Kutannusosakeyhtiö Otavan painolaitokset, 1981.

Kostiainen, Auvo. *The Forging of Finnish-American Communism, 1917–1924: A Study in Ethnic Radicalism*. Turku, Finland: Institute of Migration, 1978.

Lahti, Mr. and Mrs. Leonard. Interview by Arthur E. Puotinen, August 3, 1973. Oral history interview transcript. Finnish American Historical Archive, Finlandia University, Hancock, Michigan.

Laine, Vienna, and Jeffrey Laine. Interview by Gary Kaunonen, Escanaba, Michigan, March 23, 2007. Oral history interview, tape 1, side 2. Oral History Collection, Box 26, Finnish American Historical Archive, Finlandia University, Hancock, Michigan.

Lankton, Larry D. *Beyond the Boundaries: Life and Landscape at the Lake Superior Copper Mines, 1840–1875*. New York: Oxford University Press, 1997.

———. *From Cradle to Grave: Life, Work, and Death at Lake Superior Copper Mines*. New York: Oxford University Press, 1991.

Leary, James P. "The Legacy of Viola Turpeninen." In *Finnish Americana, Vol. 8*. New York Mills, Minn.: Parta Printers, Inc., 1990.

Lehto, Steve. *Death's Door: The Truth behind Michigan's Largest Mass Murder*. Troy, Mich.: Momentum Books, 2006.

Leiviska, Helen K. Interview by Douglas J. Ollila Jr., 1974. Oral history interview transcript. Finnish American Historical Archive, Finlandia University, Hancock, Michigan.

Lepisto, Mrs. Sigrid. Interview by Adrian A. Niemi, December, 4, 1974. Oral history interview transcript. Finnish American Historical Archive, Finlandia University, Hancock, Michigan.

Linja, Gus O. *Copper Country Connections*. Kearney, Neb.: Morris Publishing, n.d.

Loukinen, Michael. "Second Generation Finnish-American Migration from the Northwoods to Detroit, 1920–1950." In *Finnish Diaspora II: United States*. Toronto: Multicultural History Society of Ontario, 1981.

Marin, Ann. *Vernacular Architecture of Finnish Immigrants in the Central Upper Peninsula of Michigan. Unpublished* paper. December 1980 .Finnish American Historical Archive, Finlandia University, Hancock, Michigan.

Meyers, Beatrice. Interview by Gary Kaunonen and Hannu Heinilä, July 27, 2006, Chassell, Michigan. Oral history interview, nontranscribed interviews, Oral History Collection, Box 26, Finnish American Historical Archive, Finlandia University, Hancock, Michigan.

Mikkonen, Pirjo, and Sirkka Paikkala. *Sukunimet*. Helsinki, Finland: Otava, 1992.

Miller, Lynn, ed. *A Collection of Recollections: Crystal Falls, Michigan, 1880–1980*. Dallas, Tex.: Taylor Publishing Company, 1980.

Molloy, Larry. *Italian Hall: The Witnesses Speak*. Hubbell, Mich.: Great Lakes GeoScience, 2004.

National Geological Survey of Finland.http://en.gtk.fi/ExplorationFinland/Commodities/Zinc/orijarvi.html (data updated February, 15, 2006, accessed August, 2007).

Niemi, Clemens. *Americanization of the Finnish People in Houghton County, Michigan* http://www.genealogia. Fi/emi/art.article241e.htm.

Niemisto, Reuben. Interview by Allan Lavery, January 30, 1974. Oral history interview transcript. Finnish American Historical Archive, Finlandia University, Hancock, Michigan.

Niitemaa, Viljo. "The Finns in the Great Migratory Movement from Europe to America 1865-1914." In *Finland Salutes U.S.A.: Old Friends—Strong Ties*. Turku, Finland: Institute of Migration, 1976.

Ollikainen, Viktor, to Hilja Fraki, personal correspondence, January 24,1913. Hilja Fraki Collection, Manuscripts Box T-53, Finnish American Historical Archive, Finlandia University, Hancock, Michigan.

Ollila, Jr., Douglas J. "The Suomi Synod: 1890-1920." In *The Faith of the Finns: Historical Perspectives on the Finnish Lutheran Church in America*. East Lansing: Michigan State University Press, 1972.

———. "The Suomi Synod in Perspective." In *The Finns in North America: A Social Symposium*. East Lansing: Michigan State University Press, 1969.

———. "The Work People's College: Immigrant Education for Adjustment and Solidarity." In *For the Common Good: Finnish Immigrants and the Radical Response to Industrial America*. Superior, Wisc.: Tyomies Society, 1977.

O'Meara, James. Interview by Arthur Puotinen, July 13, 1972. Oral history interview transcript. Finnish American Historical Archive, Finlandia University, Hancock, Michigan.

Penti, Marsha Elizabeth. *Religious Identities in the Composition Class: Students of Difference*. PhD diss., Michigan Technological University, 1998.

Phillips, Bruce "Utah" and Ani DiFranco. "Direct Action," on *Fellow Workers*. Buffalo, N.Y.: Righteous Babe Records, 1999.

Puotinen, Arthur. "Copper Country Finns and the Strike of 1913." In *The Finnish Experience in the Western Great Lakes Region: New Perspectives*. Turku, Finland: Institute of Migration, 1975.

———. "Early Labor Organizations in the Copper Country." In *For the Common Good: Finnish Immigrants and the Radical Response to Industrial America*. 119-22,

Superior, Wisc.: Työmies Society, 1977.

———. "Transitions for Finnish-American Workers in Temple and Marketplace." Unpublished paper, December 7, 1970. Immigration History Research Center, University of Minnesota, Minneapolis, Minnesota.

Puotinen, Heino A. "Hap." *Sauna-Pukki.* Iron River, Mich.: Reporter Publishing Company, n.d.

Rahkonen, George. "The Michigan Timber Workers' Strike." *Työmies-Eteenpäin,* July 1998.

Randell, Kent. "Knights of Kaleva Collection Finding Aide." Andrew Brask Correspondence, Box 20, Manuscripts Collection, Finnish American Historical Archive, Finlandia University, Hancock, Michigan.

Ronn, Ernie. *52 Steps Underground: An Autobiography of a Miner.* Marquette, Mich.: The Center for Upper Peninsula Studies, Northern Michigan University, 2000.

Ross, Carl. "Essays on the Finnish American Community: 1865–1914, Part 2, The Finnish American Community Matures,1885–1900." Carl Ross papers, Immigration History Research Center, University of Minnesota.

Saarnivaara, Uuras. *The History of the Laestadian or Apostolic-Lutheran movement in America.* Ironwood, Mich.: National Publishing Company, 1947.

Salo, Dagne. Oral history interview. Recorded and transcribed by Alexey Golubev, Petrozavodsk, Russia, September 21, 2006. National Archive of the Republic of Karelia, Petrozavodsk, Russia.

Sarkela, Sandra. Interview by Elma Ranta, November 6, 1974. Oral history interview transcript. Finnish American Historical Archive, Finlandia University, Hancock, Michigan.

Savela Storhak, Esther, and Lynne Golden Palo. *J.A. Doelle School Album.* Self- published, n.d. Finnish American Historical Archive, Finlandia University, Hancock, Michigan.

Scandinavian Evangelical Lutheran Church Records. Finnish American Churches Box B- 3, Manuscripts Collection, Finnish American Historical Archive, Finlandia University, Hancock, Michigan.

Settlers Cooperative, Inc. *75 Years, 1917–1992.* Bruce Crossing, Mich.: Settlers Cooperative, Inc., 1992.

Smith, Ralph Henry. *A Sociological Survey of the Finnish Settlement of New York Mills, Minnesota and its Adjacent Territory, Revised.* Compiled by Darrel G. Nicholson. Minneapolis: Snellington Publishers, 2005.

State of Michigan. "Michigan Music Hall of Fame-Polka Music Category; Carl Pelonpaa Hall of Fame Membership Certification," September 24, 2006.

Suomi College. *Suomi College Academic Catalog 1986–89*. Hancock, Mich.: Suomi College, 1985.

———. *Suomi Opisto Fennia, 1915*. Hancock, Mich.: Finnish Lutheran Book Concern, 1915.

Suomi Synod Collection, Kaleva, Michigan, Manuscript Collection Boxes A-91a and A- 91b, Membership Rolls, Finnish American Historical Archive, Finlandia University, Hancock, Michigan.

Syrjälä, William. *The Reino V. and Vienna H. Laine Collection of William Syrjälä and Viola Turpeinen Materials from Jeffrey C. Laine*, Manuscripts Collection, Box Z-1a. Finnish American Historical Archive, Finlandia University, Hancock, Michigan.

Thurner, Arthur. *Strangers and Sojourners: A History of Michigan's Keweenaw Peninsula*. Detroit: Wayne State University Press, 1994.

Turunen, Evelyn. Interview by Elaine Loukinen, September 28, 1974. Oral history interview transcript. Finnish American Historical Archive, Finlandia University, Hancock, Michigan.

Työmies Publishing Company. *Vallankumous VIII: Työvaen-Opiston Toverikunnan Kevätjulkaisu 1915*. Superior, Wisc.: Työmies Publishing Company, 1915.

Työmies Society. "Early Finnish American Newspapers in U.S.A." In *Työmies: Seventieth Anniversary Souvenir Journal, 1903–1973*. Superior, Wisc.: Työmies Society, 1973.

———. "Finnish Socialist Federation" In *Työmies: Seventieth Anniversary Souvenir Journal, 1903–1973*. Superior, Wisc.: Työmies Society, 1973.

Ukkonen, Alfons. *A History of the Kaleva Knighthood and the Knights of Kaleva*. Translated by Tessa Suurkuukka. Beaverton, Ontario: Aspasia Books, 2002.

Virtanen, Keijo. "The Influence of the Automobile Industry on the Ethnic Picture of Detroit, Michigan, 1900–1940." In *Publications of the Institute of History, General History, University of Turku, Finland, No. 9*. Vaasa, Finland: Vaasan Kirjapaino Oy, 1977.

———. "Problems of Research in Finnish Re-emigration." In *The Finnish Experience in the Western Great Lakes Region: New Perspectives*. Turku, Finland: Institute of Migration, 1975.

Walli, Frank. Interview by Douglas J. Ollila, August 8, 1973. Oral history interview transcript. Finnish American Historical Archive, Finlandia University, Hancock, Michigan.

Wargelin, John. "The Finns in Michigan." *Michigan History Magazine* 24 (Spring 1940).

Wargelin Brown, K. Marianne. "Maggie Walz: Entrepreneur and Temperance Crusader." In *Women Who Dared: The History of Finnish American Women,* ed. Carl Ross and K. Marianne Wargelin Brown. St. Paul, Minn.: Immigration History Research Center, 1986.

Index